Churchill's
Legionnaire

Churchill's Legionnaire, Edmund Murray

Edmund
Murray

Edited by Bill Murray

First published in the UK by Unicorn
an imprint of the Unicorn Publishing Group LLP, 2021
5 Newburgh Street
London W1F 7RG

www.unicornpublishing.org

ISBN: 978-1-913491-25-3

Design by Vivian@Bookscribe

Printed by Gomer Press, Wales

Contents

Charles de Gaulle

Winston Churchill

Prologue

In the first week of November 1958, on his way back from a stay in the south of France, Sir Winston Churchill stopped off in Paris where he was to receive the French nation's highest honour, *La Croix de la Libération*, from the hands of his war-time 'colleague', General de Gaulle. Churchill had once described de Gaulle as the '… greatest cross that he [Churchill] had to bear…' The ceremony took place in the Matignon Gardens and Churchill stayed the night at the British Embassy where his son-in-law, Christopher Soames, was the British Ambassador. The following day, prior to departure from Orly, the General gave Sir Winston lunch at the Elysée Palace.

The lunch terminated. Churchill descended to the entrance by lift but de Gaulle marched down the elegant marble staircase. I was there preparing to assist Sir Winston by offering my arm as usual. General de Gaulle reached the last steps when Churchill turned to him and bellowed out, in understandable French but with his usual terribly English accent: '*Vous devez connaître mon garde-du-corps, le Sergent Murray… il a passé dix années dans votre Légion Etrangère.*'

The General, faced by this momentous disclosure had no other option than to come towards me with hand outstretched. I thought for a moment that he was going to salute me in the typical Gallic way with kisses on both cheeks, but he restrained himself, grasped my hand firmly and asked me when and where I had honoured the Legion with my presence. We chatted, without interruption from Churchill who just stood by watching with a smirk on his features for a good ten minutes looking like his cat at Chartwell after stealing a bit of fish, before shaking hands once again and saying goodbye. A few minutes later as we made our way with a *Garde Mobile* escort towards the airport, I turned round in my seat beside the chauffeur to thank Sir Winston for his kind gesture. I could see that he was still smiling contentedly and relishing the moment.

From this episode came the idea of calling the story of my time in the French Foreign Legion, *Churchill's Légionnaire.*

Author's Note

In my autobiography, *I was Churchill's Bodyguard,* published by W.H. Allen of London in 1987, I wrote about my life in the French Foreign Legion without really going into the matter in any great length, but used it to suggest the probable reasons for my being chosen, in 1950, to protect Sir Winston Churchill MP, then Leader of the Opposition in the House of Commons. I was deemed to be the right officer in the right place at the right time and was selected by the then Chief of Special Branch, the late Commander Leonard Burt, with the approval of the Home Secretary who was the final arbiter on such an important assignment. I was to remain with Sir Winston as his constant companion for the next fifteen years, accompanying him wherever he went on land, on sea and in the air, and even on one occasion, under the sea on a submarine with Lord Mountbatten acting as guide in the south of France. I was just outside his bedroom when he died on 24 January 1965, leaving behind an emptiness that will never be filled.

I received many wonderful letters of congratulations on my autobiography including one from Lady Churchill who wrote that I had gone over and beyond the call of duty. Mr Anthony AD Montague Browne, CBE, DFC, one of the numerous private secretaries that Winston Churchill had throughout his long public life, commented in a review of my book for the International Churchill Association, that more details about my life in the French Foreign Legion would not have gone amiss and this sentiment was echoed by many others.

So here is the book about my life in the Legion which I dedicate to my comrades, that great family of merry, mean yet magnificent mercenaries, the men of the French Foreign Legion.

Vive La France! Vive la Légion!

Edmund Murray, Bath, 30 April 1994

Foreword
by Simon Murray

This is the remarkable story of a young man in the French Foreign Legion, where he spent eight important and character-forming years of his life. Edmund Murray joined the Legion in 1937, two years before the outbreak of World War Two, and is sent to the strange world of Algeria and even stranger world of the Foreign Legion at the young age of nineteen. His early years are relatively mild as he joins the Legion band and has some 'freedoms' compared to other legionnaires, but we can see the Legion through his lucid writing, which is free of exaggeration and a pleasure to read.

When the war breaks out the band is abandoned and in 1941 he is sent to Indochina and it is war with the Japanese. His five years in Indochina take us through the head-to-head battle with ferocious Japanese fighters in the deep jungle of Vietnam. Realising that he is in his mid-twenties keeps the reader in a state of constant amazement at what he is going through.

It is also a story of friendships between allies and strangers and the essential *Esprit de Corps* that keeps the Legion, made up of 'foreigners' to each other, as the original *Band of Brothers*.

This is a must-read for young people starting out in life to whom I always say, "*Do not follow where the path may lead, but go instead where there is no path and leave a trail.*" And it makes the older generation read with envy and think "Now why didn't I do that?".

*Churchill's Legionnai*re has brought back many memories as in 1960 I followed the same path as Edmund Murray; it is a coincidence that we are both Murrays as we are not related. I also joined aged nineteen and recalled my experiences in *Legionnaire: Five Years in the French Foreign Legion*. Running off to join the French Foreign Legion is something that many have thought about but few have accomplished. The life of a Legionnaire is a unique experience – and one that is worth sharing.

1
Childhood memories

I t was in 1934 when I decided, against the wishes of my parents and teachers, to abandon the long road to university and follow my brothers to London to seek my fortune, or maybe just adventure.

After eighteen months with Joe Sainsbury as a counter-hand, a summer season as a deck-steward on the *Crested Eagle*, a paddle steamer of the General Steam Navigation Company plying between Tower Pier and Clacton-on-Sea, and a hectic twenty-eight days with the Irish Guards at Caterham, Surrey, I joined my brother Joe at the Holborn Restaurant as a checking clerk. Although I enjoyed the work there, in very pleasant company and conditions as well as the cricket outings round the London and Middlesex area and the excitement of listening to the orchestras in vogue at the time playing in the ballrooms, I was bored. One Sunday in May 1937, copying the example of Leopold the waiter in *White Horse Inn* (though my heart was not broken), I just got up and left, as I had decided to join the French Foreign Legion.

❧

I was born on 18 August 1917 in a very small mining village in County Durham. It was called Low Friarside, and I mean *was*, for when I took Beryl my wife to see it just a few months after we were married, my birthplace was no more. The fifty or so houses once all occupied by miners, all the way up a very steep, mile-long bank, were gone. What fun we had experienced on that bank during the winter months, for in those days we had snow to tell that it was winter and it used to last for two or three months. My father was most adept at making sledges for his children; I had two brothers and two sisters, the former both older than myself and the latter both younger.

The sledge I remember best of all was a solid wooden construction, about a yard long, eight inches high on rockers that had steel rods down the length of them; Old Bob the blacksmith along at the mine stables made those, probably for a pint bottle of ale.

The reason I recall that particular sledge was because on one occasion my two brothers, Tom and Joe, and I were riding down from the very top of the bank in the middle of the road for there was hardly ever any vehicular traffic about in those times. There was the occasional rag and bone merchant who was greatly in demand in those difficult days or the grocer's horse and cart or the coalman with his great big, wonderful, friendly draught horses. The animals using the roads in winter were always shod with shoes that had heavy prism-shaped spikes in them to help them to keep going on the icy surfaces.

It was a lovely evening and there was a wonderful full moon in a cloudless, dark blue sky. The Cresta Run was nothing compared to this and we sped down at what felt like hundreds of miles per hour. Just as we got to the beginning of the houses at Middle Friarside where the ground levelled off somewhat, the sledge hit something in the road and stopped dead. But we didn't stop for we were very 'posh' and always had a bit of carpet or mat to sit on. We carried on, just the mat and ourselves for many yards afterwards till friction stopped the mat and the Murray lads. One of my brothers always sat in the front with a skate on his foot to guide us without having to use our heels and toes to steer. This was the reason why we were always the fastest sledge in the district. I must have been seven or eight years old at the time and life must have been very hard for some, but oh how happy I was and how I loved those good old days and still enjoy the memory of them. My thirst for adventure clearly began at a young age.

Naturally, my father and two elder brothers worked in the mines. There was a mine at the Lintz and yet my father and eventually both brothers, still worked at the Beaumont right down at the bottom of the mile-long Friarside Bank. What torture it must have been for them to have to climb it after eight to ten hours of hewing and putting coal, miles under the hill in seams that were only 18 inches high a good part of the time. (Hewing was the cutting of the coal from the face and putting, the heaving of the loosened coal into the tubs). Tallies (round metal numbered discs) were attached to filled tubs indicating the identity of the putter, and the more tubs filled, the more the team earned. I do remember that my brothers, working together most of the time as a team acquired a superb reputation for production. My father, who had served his apprenticeship in the harder jobs during his younger days, was by now more or less comfortably placed as he did not have to hew the coal out of the seams, nor put it into the four-wheeled tubs which were drawn by the very small Shetland ponies. However, he did have the great responsibility of the wellbeing of hundreds of men on his shoulders, especially when he had to place and fire the shots that could bring down tons of rock and stone on them if the gelignite was misused or misplaced or mistimed.

He was also the one who had *to take the can back* if anything went wrong in the actual working of the mine when the gaffer (the Under-Manager) was not there, and sometimes the gaffer knew 'nowt aboot the pit' and that placed an unfair burden on his shoulders. Dad had a fixed weekly pay but often earned more by working overtime which was so often necessary when trouble arose.

When Dad and my brothers were home, the dirt and grime caked on them by the sweat of their toiling had to be washed off in a small galvanised tin bath placed in front of the fire range and filled with hot water using a ladle, as baths and showers in miners' houses were quite unknown in those days. Nowadays of course, miners go to work in suits, changing and showering at the pithead which is most civilised, and who could possibly say that they do not deserve it.

These days when explosions or roof falls occur in mines around the world, they are reported by the media and rewards are often handed out to those brave men who save, or try to save, the injured and recover the bodies of those who have not made it. But in those days of the 1930s and before, only those involved knew about the terrible calamities that happened; of the men killed or injured, of the women and children deprived of husbands and fathers, and there was never, or only rarely, any reward for miners risking their lives for their fellows. It was only after his death that our family found proof, in the shape of medals and testaments, of valorous actions of our father. When miners talked about their mines and heroic deeds, it was always someone else who had been brave, not themselves.

How my mother, Margaret Buchanan Gibson Wildsmith Murray became endowed with such a fine name, with such Scottish connotations, I have not been able to find out, but she was a wonderful mother. They made them like that in mining districts, their one thought being for their family even though they must have found it very difficult in those days to make ends meet. Oh yes! I have heard Meggie, as she was known to her peers, sigh at the injustices in the world; I've heard her threaten me with the direst of punishments for misdemeanours; I've felt her hand across my cheek very often for some misdeed or another, but there was always concern and love in her eyes when one or other of us was ill or suffering from some wound, for, as the song goes, that we sang so often, and I still do: *The angels above, taught the way how to love, to that old fashioned mother of mine.*

Part of our small house was set out as a sweet shop, the only one in the hamlet. I can remember the big glass jars filled with gobstoppers, jelly babies, Liquorice Allsorts and liquorice sticks in the window facing the road and can see in my mind's eye the vegetable garden at the back. When Mother gave up the shop she used to say that it was because I ate all the chocolates.

My maternal grandmother lived in Grosvenor Street in Gateshead, now long gone of course for Gateshead has much changed and perhaps once a month, on a Saturday, we would all walk to Gateshead. The whole Wildsmith clan always seemed to sense that we were going there and turned up as well in time for tea and home-made bread and scones and jam. This was always most mysterious because the telephone was unheard of in private homes and not much letter writing took place either. Dad used to take along the mandolin, Uncle Bill from Forest Hall (he was Will to us and my father was Will to them) which was a few miles on the Whitley Bay and Tynemouth side of Newcastle, would bring along his concertina and his bones and there would be several kazoos and combs with pieces of greaseproof paper. After tea someone older would go along to the off-licence and return with beer and then we would have a musical evening, very frequently interrupted with arguments about anything at all. But there was never any real vitriol and most of the time we were all laughing and having fun.

My brothers and I attended the Leazes School where Mr Dick Abbott was the Headmaster for many years. He was a fair man, handing out punishment only when he considered it necessary. I remember vividly one occasion when he caned me. The cane was about 30 inches long being perhaps an inch in diameter at one end tapering to a blunt point at the other. It was not a very flexible cane and it hurt when it was applied with the usual fervour by the Headmaster – and by no-one else. On this occasion I had received perhaps three of the six I was due when the cane broke in the middle. Mr Abbott said that I was lucky for fate had decreed what had happened and the remainder were waived. But all in all, I was a good pupil receiving several books as presents at the end of term for coming top of the class. Between Standards 4 and 5, when I was ten years old, with Misses Robinson and Whalen respectively as my teachers, I won a full scholarship to Grammar school and the wonderful world of education was wide open for me.

Life at Grammar school was, to say the least of it, not very inspiring to begin with, but then I began to adapt and realised that my parents had gone to a lot of trouble to fit me out, albeit with second-hand goods, with the blazer, tie, cap with red button on top to denote that I was a member of the Dunelm House, grey flannels and black shoes that were *de rigueur* at Alderman Wood School, West Stanley. It was a mixed school, with many of the girls' and boys' parents in commerce or business and quite well-off according to north-country standards. Quite a number of them looked down their noses at the son of a miner and it took me quite a while to come to terms with this sort of behaviour.

Though I was obliged to be very much a loner because of the lack of funds, occasionally I was invited to accompany a couple of local lads on our bikes to Dipton, a few miles away, to make up the numbers so to speak, if they had arranged to meet girls who went to our school. Going to the cinema was out of the question mainly because of the expense of transport, and in those days if I had any money, I preferred to play snooker, either just over the garden fence at the Community Hall – 20 minutes for a penny – or in the Snooker Hall at West Stanley with my older friend Jim Burrows.

Out of school I was of course a member of the 1st Tanfield Scout Group but as there were not very many of us, I really spent more time with the older Rover Troop of which my brother Tom was a member. It was fun and we had many very interesting trips and camps though it always seemed to rain at our regular Easter weekend. I have many happy memories of those early scouting days when I used to wear a real scout hat, almost indistinguishable from the regulation issue, but which I had inherited somehow from my Uncle Tom who had seen service in the British Legion of Frontiersmen in South Africa. I wore it when I attended the Scout Jamboree at Gosforth Park, near Newcastle, in the 1930s when I had the great fortune to shake hands with Lord Baden-Powell, the founder of the Scout movement, together with another two thousand or so scouts who were also in attendance there.

I also organised my own little group of lads of my own age at Tantobie. I cannot remember what we called ourselves but we had badges depicting a Red Indian and it was all according to rules and regulations set down in my favourite reading matter at the time, *Boys Magazine*, which cost two-pence a week. However, I used to walk to Stanley on Saturdays, it was a good couple of miles, and in the market I could purchase perhaps a half dozen old copies for two or three pence. We used to go out to the fells, half a mile away from the houses where some quarrying had been done a long time before, and play cowboys and Indians. Such happy, carefree days.

On Tuesday evenings, my brother Tom and I rode regularly to Gateshead to train in a Gymnasium run by Seaman Watson, one-time cruiser-weight champion of Great Britain. About that time, I was thinking of taking up boxing seriously, but during a workout in the cricket pavilion at Tantobie where we were also receiving instruction from a former boxer-cum-miner, Bill Bailey, my brother smashed a right full on to my heart and I was out for several minutes. I then gave up any ideas of taking up boxing professionally, but the experience I gained has served me well since.

We three brothers used to play for the Tantobie cricket team and I remember real summers, with weeks and weeks of lovely weather with only the occasional match rained off. I feel sure my brothers paid my subscription and for my teas and it was never mentioned, but then family was family and kindness never-failing.

It was not surprising that brother Joe decided in the early thirties, after the disastrous strike and the famous Jarrow March, to seek his fortune in London. Tom then made up his mind to leave mining and also moved to London where he joined the Police Force. And it was not long before I too decided to follow my brothers and moved to London for a few years and multiple jobs. Eventually, my restlessness took over. And so it was that on a beautiful Sunday morning at the beginning of May, at about seven o'clock in the morning, with the sun shining brightly and the birds singing merrily as they flew to and from Hampstead Heath, I set off for a new life. Not wishing to wake my brother Joe with whom I shared a flat at 27 Gayton Road, I had partaken of no breakfast, intending to get a sandwich at Victoria station. It was a wonderful world. I was off to join the French Foreign Legion.

2
The Long Road to Algeria

I had been working as a checking clerk at the Holborn Restaurant, one of the finest restaurants in London when I upped and left to join the Legion. I would sit at the top of a flight of steps leading down into the Balcony kitchen where Monsieur Rolland held sway. He was a lovely Frenchman speaking excellent English with a very marked French accent. He was six feet tall and must have weighed twenty stone. His face was always a lovely rosy colour and it was not really because of the heat of the kitchen for he could not cook without his bottle of red wine close to him. He was a most remarkable *ma tre chef* who turned out the most glorious *cuisine;* I learned a lot from Monsieur Rolland. One Saturday I went to Rolland just as the day was closing and I told him that I would not be in on Monday and would probably be replaced by my brother Joe and would Monsieur Rolland tell him that I had gone to join the French Foreign Legion. He was quite horrified and did his best to persuade me, as a Frenchman who knew what he was talking about, to give up the idea and stay at the Holborn where I was a respected employee, probably in the line for swift promotion for I was young and already had my first foot on the ladder. I would think about it, I told him with my tongue in my cheek knowing full well that I had made the decision and would stick to it. We kissed goodbye anyhow, and I am so glad we did for I heard after my return ten years later that he had committed suicide at the beginning of the war. Reasons were not known.

So, the following morning, dressed in grey sports jacket and grey flannels, collar and tie, and with about £5 in my pocket and a total absence of any luggage, I had not a care in the world as I marched off towards Victoria station to catch the boat train leaving at 10.00 am.

It must have been a very uneventful trip for I do not remember anything about it, until I landed in Boulogne. I know that I had no passport nor travel documents, just my return ticket. Yet I recall getting to the Police station and enquiring about joining the French Foreign Legion. Thanks to Miss 'Frenchie' Butters and Miss Boyd at school, my French, judged by my teachers as pretty poor, suddenly became important and sufficient and I soon learned that there was no recruiting office in Boulogne. The nearest centre for the Legion was at St Omer, some thirty miles to the east and the next bus was not due to leave for a couple of hours. I had time for lunch.

Looking for a place to eat, I soon found a small bistrot, went in and asked if they took English money, which they did. I sat down and consumed a wonderful steak with chips and salad, washed down with, and I'm not really ashamed to confess, a glass of water for I did not drink in those days. The lady who was in charge, the *patronne*, then asked me a few questions and I told her that I still had a good hour to wait for the bus. She suggested that I might like company and disappeared for a few minutes returning with a lovely young lady, perhaps a couple of years my senior. She sat down at my table and had a glass of wine. There appeared to be no charge.

Then, to my surprise, Madame displaced a column of empty cardboard boxes hiding a door in the corner of the bar and the young lady took me by the hand and led me to a small, very neat room at the top of the stairs. I then began to suspect what was going to happen, especially when she asked me for money. Another one of my precious pounds left my possession. Were I writing for certain publications I would go into details, but as this is being written for the nicest possible readers, proved by letters from all over the world after the publication of my first book, I shall just say that it seemed that a good time was had by all. Before leaving I asked Madame to change a pound note into French francs for me and then found my way to the bus station and the conveyance that was due to leave soon for St Omer.

I paid my fare and boarded, sitting at the front so that I could see everything that went on before me. We eventually started off across the battlefields of French Flanders and the bus kept filling up with people, hens, ducks, two pigs and cockerels calling to each other. They all seemed to realise that there was a foreigner on the bus for the other passengers were all in their working clothes, farmers or market-sellers, and I being the only one dressed comparatively smartly. I was the only one also who did not smell of garlic, or sausage, or coffee, or the droppings of the other things being carried to the market at St Omer which is the local capital city of the Calais Department. It was awful, or so I thought at the time, but I have become quite immune to the smells of France since and have indeed come to love them. I realise now, looking back, that each foreign country – or perhaps each foreign city – that I have ever visited had its own particular smell, and each one quite different to our own. The bus was so old that it must have seen service during the First World War.

Once deposited at St Omer I went to the Gendarmerie and asked the usual question about joining up. They directed me to the Recruiting Office which was in the local barracks. There, they actually found a soldier who spoke reasonable English; we seemed to be on the same wavelength and got on very well. We had supper together in an office and then I was shown to a dormitory where I spent the night with about twenty other soldiers who tried to dissuade me from joining that 'bloody awful regiment of criminals'. They thought that I was funny for not drinking wine for they brought out a couple of bottles just to be friendly. When they had finished them we all turned in. I was very tired, still very hungry, but very happy and I slept extremely well until *Reveille* at 6 am. We had coffee, a chunk of French bread with two sardines and a piece of very dark chocolate for breakfast. My new friend then took me along to the Adjutant's office and after giving details of my parents' address, of my last job, and a few other things, I was sent away with my soldier friend to have coffee, and then later on, lunch, before returning to the office about four hours later.

The Adjutant got me to sign papers, a contract really with the French Minister of War to the effect that I would faithfully serve France and the Legion for a first minimum period of five years. It was done.

The next morning, after a cup of coffee and a dry piece of bread with two more sardines, my friend handed me a bag containing what he called my lunch. He then took me along to the station and eventually put me on a train for Toul where he said I would be met. He wished me good luck and hoped that I would not be disappointed with what the future held for me. We shook hands and I took stock of my carriage. I was all alone in a wooden cabin which could seat perhaps eight or ten people on wooden varnished benches. The compartment was quite clean but I found the bench rather hard. The carriage had been locked, I suddenly realised, to keep me there but I had absolutely no intention of trying to get out as the train moved off on its way towards Toul.

The weather continued to be very warm as I went on my nearly three hundred-mile trip. My friend had given me a paper bag containing my lunch but I was not hungry. The countryside through which I was travelling was much too lovely to be missed. Farms were busy places in those days, rivers and canals were used, petrol fumes did not pollute the air and the window was open so I did not feel sleepy at all. God was in His Heaven and all was right with the world until there crept upon me a feeling that all was not well. A smell began to permeate through the carriage and it was not a very pleasant smell.

My first thought was that a dead rat was sharing the compartment with me, but as the train rattled on I became convinced that it was a dead cat, or even a horse so offensive did the stink become. I had to do something about it, for I felt that I was about to perish, so I brought into use that splendid organ with which I was endowed and went sniffing round the carriage, first in the corners, then on the rack above me, then under the seat, but everything was quite clean and open to my scrutiny, till I came upon that paper bag containing my *casse-croûte*. Surely not, I thought to myself. We all know of the French and their thoughts about *les Anglais* but they would never descend to such an odious trick as to put a dead something in my lunch bag! But there was no doubt about it, the smell, the stench, did actually emanate from the paper bag. I opened it to investigate; there was no corpse, only half a military loaf, a bar of chocolate, an apple and an orange, and a round box of paper-thin white wood. I lifted the lid on which I deciphered the word *Camembert* and immediately threw the offending box out of the window, then began to relax in the rapidly sweeter-smelling carriage. I munched the chocolate and dry bread, washed down with mouthfuls of sweet coffee from the *bidon* which was to stay with me for many weeks to come. It was a pity, I thought, that whatever it was they had given me for lunch had gone off before I had even sampled it.

In the years to come I was to become more or less addicted to that loveliest of French cheeses, the Camembert, and how often have I wished that I could stretch out my hand to recover the jewel I threw out of the window of my railway carriage, *en route* for Toul.

Waiting on the platform, just where my carriage ended up, was a Sergeant with two gold chevrons on his sleeve and two légionnaires by his sides, armed with sheathed bayonets. He asked me if I was Légionnaire Edmond Murray (pronounced Miouray) and I concurred and off we marched through the streets of Toul to the barracks with me positioned between the two légionnaires. No interrogations took place here. There were about twelve of us in the one bed-cum-dining-room and we just ate and drank and they all seemed to like wine, but I still preferred water or coffee.

We stayed there for a couple of days then off we were marched to the station to catch the train for Marseilles, many miles and many dreary hours away. We were all still in civilian clothes and escorted by a Sergeant and two légionnaires, again armed with bayonets, indicating I suppose, the type of person they usually expected to be escorting.

On our arrival in Marseilles, we were marched down to the Old Port and the Canebière, the main artery of the city's life, and along to Fort St Jean, guardian of the old harbour, where we were incarcerated for the next week or so until there was room on the SS *Gouverneur Général de Gueydon* in the lowest deck compartments usually reserved for cattle.

In Fort St Jean, where there were perhaps fifty or more recruits and veteran légionnaires who saw to the normal duties of the barracks which could not be entrusted to new entrants, I began to understand that we were now members of a hard-working organisation. A new *foyer* was being built on the level of the barracks, hundreds of feet above the street and water level for the fort is right on the edge of the harbour. This meant climbing numerous flights of stone steps that had been worn down by centuries of use by military footwear, laden with the huge blocks of quarried stone for the building. The *foyer* is the French equivalent of our British NAAFI (Navy, Army and Air Force Institute). I had never been engaged in hard manual work before and during the ten days that we were there I found my hands progressed from being sore, to being bloody sore, then incredibly painful, to being gnarled and immune to further pain from the harsh treatment.

One day the group with which I had come from Toul were ordered to congregate on the small parade ground in front of the barracks. We were dressed in light khaki knee-breeches, jacket, puttees and army boots, some parts of which fitted more or less, while others were ridiculously too small or too large. We were not to be issued with the famous Legion *képi* until much later, after we had finished our military instruction and become real légionnaires or considered to be such, and so at this time we wore forage caps. I was reasonably happy with my outfit for the French Army seemed to favour the taller type of soldier rather than the smaller one for their Government issue. We took along, as instructed, our civilian effects and these were duly auctioned off, without any reference to the owners, to civilians who had been invited to attend. The amounts received were later handed to us – less a reduction for undisclosed reasons – and we had to sign for the money we received. Argument was apparently out of the question as I was informed by a new-found friend who spoke excellent English, a Dutchman named Reyst (this could have been his real name) whose Legion warrant number was 71823 while mine was 71824. These numbers had been given to us when we were issued with our make-do uniforms and we had to mark our effects with our respective numbers thenceforth with indelible ink pencil. Reyst was to accompany me for many weeks afterwards and he often acted as my interpreter when the Legion French became too complicated. Our ways parted after instruction at Saïda in Algeria but I shall be forever grateful to him.

The system for transporting soldiers across the seas never changed, whether it was across the Mediterranean, or as I discovered later, via the Atlantic Ocean, the Indian Ocean, or the South China Sea. Two, or even three-tiered bunks were set up solidly in the bowels of the ship and that was that. However long the journey, the Legion took over the cleaning and the security of the vessel, fire drills two or three times a day, physical exercise at 6am and 6pm and marching up and down the cleared decks was also organised, just to keep us all fit. We crossed from Marseilles to Oran in 24 hours on the *Gouverneur Général de Gueydon* to be received by the only American-born officer of the Legion I ever met, one Captain Hamilton. We only had a very brief chat before being shoved on to the train which was to take us to Sidi-bel-Abbès, the famous headquarters of the French Foreign

Legion. We were not staying in Sidi-bel-Abbès but simply passing through to Saïda where we were to receive our basic training – or instruction as it was known – thirteen weeks of sheer hard work to determine whether we were really cut out for a life in the Legion. I noticed immediately that Algeria had a different smell to France or Britain. It was dry and it smelled of sand and palms, French tobacco and *kuskus*. I was very interested. I wanted to get stuck into my new life; to receive my uniform, to march off into the wilderness that separates the cultivated areas of Algeria from the real Sahara Desert, for after all, that was why I had joined the Legion.

3
Giving Oneself to the Legion

France has always welcomed foreigners to fight for her – I say this in the nicest possible way for few would question the renown of French national armies on the battlefield – and those who have served her have always been just as welcome to remain as citizens of France afterwards.

King Phillipe Auguste, (1165–1223) bought in bands of roving foot soldiers to fight against England's own Henry II and to follow him to the Crusades. He recruited Irishmen, Germans, Italians, and even Scots. Then in 1418, King Charles VII of France (1403–1461), founded the *Garde Ecossaise*, an elite Scottish military unit. These men became the personal bodyguards of the French monarchy and fought against the English and Henry VI. And whilst I indulge in some historical facts, here is another: the French National Anthem bears the name of a lady inhabitant of the remarkable city of Marseilles, and yet the song does not originate from there. Both words and music were composed to all intents and purposes, during the night of 24 April in 1792, in Strasbourg, by a Captain of Engineers who dabbled in music. He was Claude Joseph Rouget de Lisle to whom the then Mayor of Strasbourg had suggested that the French required a rousing marching song. De Lisle was in barracks in Strasbourg at the time and he worked through the night to please the Mayor and the hymn was born. It was only when it was sung so enthusiastically by troops and citizens setting out from Marseilles for Paris during the Revolution that the title *La Marseillaise* was adopted. The work undoubtedly underwent improvement, probably by Grétry and Gossec, as time passed before it reached its existing form. Subsequent pitiful attempts to change certain bloodthirsty expressions in the anthem during the early 1990s failed miserably.

So there we have it. Not only does *La Marseillaise* come from outside of Marseille; many of France's brave soldiers have come from outside France's borders. However, it was Louis Philippe, Duke of Orleans, Duke of Provence who, on becoming citizen-king in 1830, made things official with a Royal Decree which set out the founding of the French Foreign Legion. The Royal Decree was signed on 9 March 1831.

Europe was in turmoil and the new formation, to be used outside the Kingdom of France, rapidly became the refuge of men from countries undergoing revolution and injustice. It became the home for men without a home and since the beginning, engagements in the Legion could be accepted without proof of identity.

Once the Legion had been formed, it began to figure very prominently and gloriously in every theatre of war where France was involved – Algeria, Morocco, Spain, Crimea, Italy, Mexico, Indochina, South Africa, Sudan, Madagascar, Tunisia, Germany, Syria and Norway. There was never a hint of disrepute as far as fighting and bravery were concerned; no abandonment of mission, no surrender without honour, only glory and devotion to France and to the Legion.

But it was not just fighting and battles that the Legion became known for. These men with no names tamed the wild and inhospitable deserts of north Africa. Most people when conjuring up an image of the desert think of it as a vast expanse of lovely sand like one sees at the seaside in England, but this is so incorrect. The Sahara starts in the foothills of the Atlas Mountains and the northern area of Algeria is part of the *reg* composed of wind-scoured plains, strewn with gravel, pebbles and boulders, as compared with the *erg* which is the desert of shifting sand dunes lying at the bottom of the great basins where ancient rivers piled up most alluvium. This latter part of the Sahara, which incidentally comes from the Arabic word *sahra* meaning wilderness, comprises the major part of the 3½ million square miles of the desert which stretches from the Atlantic Ocean to the Red Sea, and is seldom less than 1,000 miles wide from north to south. The *hammada* are the rocky plateaux with bare outcrops often cut into by deep valleys and gorges found around Ahaggar and Tibesti in the central southern areas, and at lower altitudes in the Western Sahara. It is inhospitable and yet it is into these wild places of north Africa that the Legion, and the Légionnaires, for many years, have been drawn.

It all started in June 1830, when General de Bourmont landed with his army at the little peninsula of Sidi-Ferruch, sixteen miles west of Algiers. He chased away the barbaresque pirates, in his words: '[to] bring back the liberty of the seas'. The coast of France was only 500 miles away but, after the fall of the Roman Empire this was a land of feuds between *çofs* or clans, invasions by pirates, deadly famines and pestilent epidemics. Bourmont told his soldiers: 'The cause of France is that of humanity. Show yourselves worthy of your noble mission. Be just and humane'. Then he declared to the inhabitants of that state, later to be called Algeria:

The practice of the Mohammedan religion will remain free. The liberty of all classes, their religion, their properties, their trades and their industries will not be harmed. Their persons will be respected.

Lyautey, Jonnart, Galliéni and other great French colonials have always proclaimed the same ideals and have acted accordingly, 'to colonise is to civilise' or was in those days.

In Algeria it was estimated, rather arbitrarily, that there were 2 million inhabitants in 1830. Today there are certainly more than 10,000,000 including 2.5 million in the city of Algiers alone. Until Algerian independence in July 1962, the development of the country was largely due to the contributions from four professions, and this is where the Legion really came into force. The soldier, the engineer, the farmer and the doctor were all vital, starting with the work of the solider and the engineer – roles in which the légionnaires excelled.

The soldiers forced peace upon the tribes that were always in conflict with each other so they felt somewhat safe. With security came cultivation and regular harvests, putting an end to periodic famines and epidemics; the engineers complemented the work of the soldier by laying out roads and railways, designing drainage canals, dams and irrigation canals. They were then built by the armies. The farmer fertilised the land left fallow by the natives who were then brought in to participate in the work and shown, by example, how to improve their existence. Then French doctors, army and civilian, often at the cost of their lives, brought to the native population the great benefit of their qualities and scientific achievement honouring the oath they swore when they first took up their profession.

One such example was the army doctor, Alphonse Laveran, who, in November 1880, discovered the parasite of malaria; not a *miasma* as was commonly thought, but a real microbe and thus began a new era of exotic pathology opening the way for research into mysterious diseases conveyed by insects. It was revolutionary. Of course, the native populations had, and still have, great confidence in the remedies of their forefathers: herbs and superstitious customs still prevail in some parts, for example a sick person being made to swallow a piece of paper on which has been written some verse by a *marabout* (Moslem holy man), or a black hen being boiled with its feathers still on then put in an old clay pot before being placed, on a dark night, in the middle of a nearby road. Whoever, whether on foot, in a car or cart, or on some other form of transport, displaced the pot to

LEGION ETRANGERE

HONNEUR   VALEUR

ET   ET

FIDÉLITÉ   DISCIPLINE

Extrait de l'Ordre
PARTICULIER

N°   6

du   24 Août   1945

LE GENERAL DE DIVISION SABATTIER, COMMANDANT
SUPERIEUR DES TROUPES FRANCAISES EN CHINE,
Vu le Décret du 4 Avril 1945
Vu le Télégramme d'Etat n° 899/DN en date du
9 Avril 1945,

CITE A L'ORDRE DU REGIMENT

MURRAY Edmund, n° d'Inc. 71.284, Sergent du 2ème Batail
------------- lon du 5ème Régiment Etranger d'Infanterie.

" Sous-Officier très brave au feu. Au cours "
" du combat du 1er Mai 1945, a commandé son groupe avec "
" un grand calme, le maintenant sur une position prise "
" sous un feu puissant et rapproché, pour assurer le re- "
" pli difficile de son unité. N'a évacué la position "
" qu'au moment où il risquait d'être complètement encer- "
" clé. "

LA PRESENTE CITATION COMPORTE L'ATTRIBUTION DE
LA CROIX DE GUERRE 1939-1945 AVEC ETOILE EN BRONZE

Pour copie conforme :
Sidi-Abbès, le 12 Décembre 1947
Le Colonel   GAULTIER
Commandant le Dépôt Commun
des Régiments Etrangers

P.O. LE LT-COLONEL NICOLAS, CDT.
EN SECOND

Citation for Award of Croix de Guerre
(Author's Collection)

Edmund Murray Medals
(Author's Collection)

Badge of the Foreign Legion Association
of Great Britain
(Author's Collection)

Veterans of Indochina Badge
(Author's Collection)

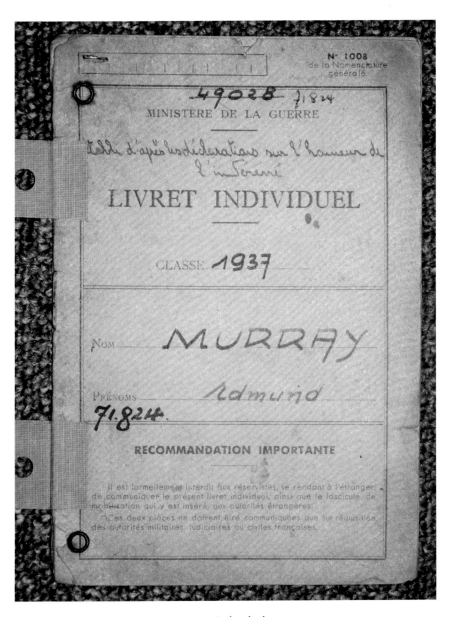

Livret Individuel
(Author's Collection)

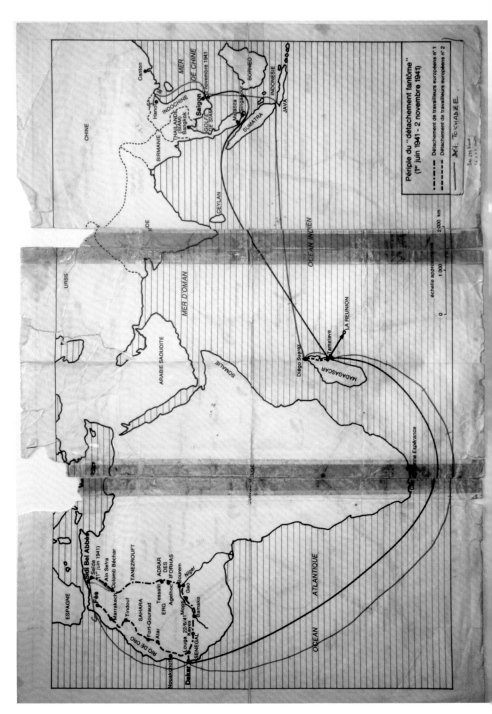

Route of Voyage from Casablanca to Indochina
(Author's Collection)

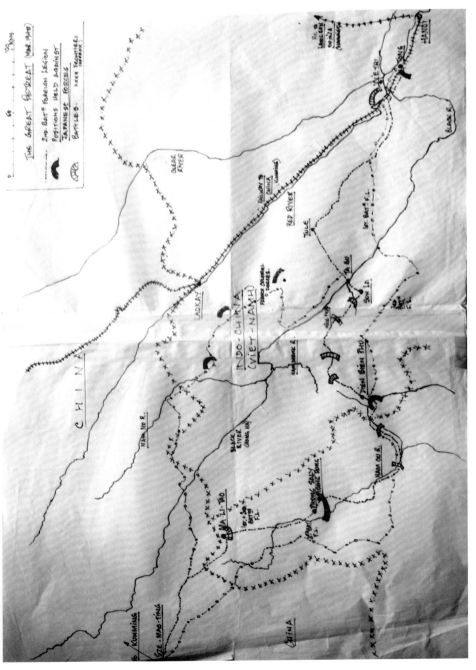

Map of the Long Retreat, 1945
(Author's Collection)

RIFLE
MOD. 1886-1893
MODIFIED 1916

"CEINTURE BLEUE"
BLUE COTTON BODY BELT
ONCE WORN TO PREVENT
STOMACH COMPLAINTS
NOW MAINLY
DECORATIVE.

MARCHING KIT
1937-41
NORTH AFRICA
1ST. REGIMENT.

E.M.

Marching Kit, French Foreign Legion, North Africa 1937–41
(Author's Collection)

ABOVE: *Murray (left) in Sidi-bel-Abbes 1937. (Kepi Blanc May 1997)*
(Author's Collection)

With love and few wishes from in Foreign Legion. Eddie September 3rd 1939.

LEFT: *Murray 1939*
(Author's Collection)

Musicians Vandam, Murray and Lance Sergeant Vilaers at the Musique in Sidi-bel-Abbas (Author's Collection)

Murray (back centre) with RAF visitors 1939
(Author's Collection)

spill its contents would inherit the complaint of the sick person who was thus delivered from it. But Algeria is a vast country covering more than 855,000 square miles, and doctors, French or Algerian, were few and far between. So, when the doctor went on his rounds he was always welcome in the isolated *douars,* greeted by the barking of dogs and the opening of doors; faces lit up and the sick brought along; spleens were tapped upon in the search for malaria; eyes examined for trachoma; blood tests were taken, injections and inoculations made, minor surgery undertaken, cauterisations done and medicines distributed. Each treatment was accepted with serious, non-smiling thanks. The doctor would be offered fruit, coffee or tea before leaving with the usual salutation *Abqaou a 'la kheir* (Stay with the good) while the crowd would respond *Roh bel a'fia* (Go in peace).

In most légionnaires there is a hunger to build something, anything. It is just something that is there in these men, uprooted from their birthplaces and without names, an instinct to which the only answer is the placing of one stone on another. In succession, légionnaires have been obliged to be warriors, peace-makers, constructors, pioneers, backwoods settlers, farmers and even, on occasions, archaeologists among other things. At the beginning of the conquest of Algeria, when first Algiers became a town, many roads from it were built by the Legion while they constructed the fortified camp of Aratch. The work they did there served as a model for the other regiments in Africa. Arriving on the scene where work was to be begun, the légionnaires formed *faisceaux* (piles) with their rifles and took up their picks and shovels.

Most of the fountains and drainage systems of Oran, the foundations and fortifications of Orléansville and those of the Legion's own city of Sidi-bel-Abbès were works of the Legion. As archaeologists, many Roman and Byzantine buried cities were uncovered by the Legion in north Africa and in Syria. As prospectors, the 24th Company of the 6th Battalion of the 1st Regiment of the Legion discovered coal in the southern Oran district.

Construction of roads, houses, fortifications, bridges, etc. held no secrets for the muscled men of the Legion performing their tasks in silence, intelligently, vigorously with their tattooed torsos tanned brown by the sun.

Protected by sentinels on dominating points, with rifles or muskets within reach, the légionnaires stripped to the waist and waded into the job that was to be done. Files of their comrades brought along great stones, or barrow-loads of pebbles, from local quarries where they had been dug out by other unskilled légionnaires. Muleteers hurried their mules along bearing water from well or stream to mix with dry earth to make *bengali* (mortar) for the bricks, handmade on the site.

The majority of roads in Algeria and Morocco had been made by the Legion and were of stone chips pounded inch by inch, foot by foot, mile by mile, not covered by tarmacadam, but dusty earth and sand. When the road came to a mountain, the sappers of the Legion made a tunnel for it to go through; when rivers or *oueds* (water-courses) were reached, bridges were built and such works, completed many years ago, still remain as memorials to the men who died from attacks by the enemy, or from illness.

It was the 4th Regiment that built the extraordinary Tizi- N'Tichka road which began at Marrakech, the place of their headquarters, and stretched along the mountainsides for almost 140 miles to Ouarzazate, having crossed the Atlas Mountains by making a pass at an altitude of 2,160m (7,087ft). I remember telling Sir Winston Churchill about this feat when we went to Tinghir in the 1950s. He was most interested. A plaque at the entrance to the tunnel states:

This tunnel was pierced through the mountain in six months (1927–1928) by only 40 légionnaires (they are all named) through the strength of their muscles and their indomitable will.

When I arrived in Algeria in May 1937, aged nineteen, it was over 100 years since the first French soldiers had set foot there and the formidable reputation of the Legion was well-established. I was excited to take my place in this extraordinary community.

4

Instruction at Saïda

I arrived in Saïda for thirteen weeks of basic instruction. Now that I was really in the Legion *ambiance* I began to learn just how much France had depended on the Legion to win Algeria and how much she depended on that same Legion to keep it. I felt proud to be a part of the force that was there to do just that and entered into the spirit of the business. A lot of our days were spent out in the *bled* (wild countryside) building roads. To begin with it was absolute torture but after a while most of us began to enjoy the slavery which we knew was not going to last forever.

Lorry-loads of large grey stones were dumped at designated spots ready for our arrival loaded with picks, shovels and a tool consisting of a long handle set into a very heavy metal round plate about 10 inches in diameter used for banging down on the stones in the road to press them down solid. In those early days I was called a *plumitif* (pen-pusher) because of the softish state of my hands, though they had suffered somewhat carrying heavy stones up those dangerous steps at Fort Saint Nicholas in Marseilles when we were building the Foyer. Using pick and shovel to dig into the very hard, sun-baked earth did cause me much pain and suffering. The old-timers told me to urinate on the blisters and scrapes and I must say that my hands got very hard in no time at all.

Some of my colleagues who divested themselves of their shirts while they did the navvying, really suffered from sunburn for days on end until their skins became immune to the burning. But this was not for me for I had too much respect for the African sun. One of the first men I met was an enormous barrel-chested Irishman called Cavanagh and I remember him being prawn-coloured for quite a few weeks and I cannot recall his ever being really tanned but I never heard him complain about sunburn. He confessed to having spent some time in English prisons which could have done little to prepare him for solar exposure. There were a number of the weaker men who suffered from sunstroke and were hospitalised but, though they might have had it easy for a while in hospital, they never really got away with it and harder work and extra *corvées* would be waiting for them when they returned to normal duties.

According to my present doctors, exposure to the sun has had a very long-lasting effect on my hands for I suffer from *solar keratoses,* a pre-cancerous skin complaint which is a blooming nuisance and most unsightly in my eyes though nobody else seems to notice.

Reveille was at 5.30am and the duty man in a barrack room had to be ready before then to dash to the kitchen with his tin *cruche* to collect the coffee with a chit made out by the Corporal or 1st class soldier in charge of the room. Then back to the men who in the meantime had been carrying out their ablutions and arranging their belongings on the shelf that ran right round the room on the wall behind their beds. This had to be done to as near perfection as possible with rectangular boards measuring probably about fourteen by four inches inserted into uniform jackets, trousers and top-coats so as to present a smart tableau for the inspecting NCOs or, on occasions, the Officers. Any untidiness would incur the destruction of the tableau and probably some other minor punishment unless it became a regular occurrence when *salle de police* or firmer measures would ensue. Beds and blankets had to receive similar treatment so there was never much time to hang about on mornings. Trousers had been pleated before going to bed and placed very carefully under the mattress. Sundays were slightly different when *Reveille* was a little later and more latitude was given as far as arranging packs and the room were concerned.

With the coffee came breakfast consisting of a thick wedge of bread, made in the garrison bakery, and a piece of hard plain chocolate, a hard-boiled egg, a piece of smoked fish or a couple of sardines. Military bread loaves were baked in the form of an empty circle measuring twelve to fourteen inches across with the hole in the middle being about four or five inches in diameter. I often wondered why they were made in this shape and eventually came to the conclusion that a normal rectangular loaf like we know them would have to be quite large and unwieldy to have the same content, so not only did they take up less room in the oven than other shapes, but they could be carried much more easily on the handlebars of bicycles when fetched by orderlies. One légionnaire would be on room duties and would have to get rid of everybody as quickly as possible so that he could wash the floor and tidy up the room before inspection. If any man had put his name down to see the doctor, or was exempt parades or training because of illness, or strained or broken bones, for instance, then he was usually detailed for room duty and would not have to do normal training.

It is interesting to note that the old British Army 'spit and polish' method of creating a mirror-like finish to boots, especially the toe-caps, is also *de rigueur* in the French Foreign Legion.

Corporals or even first-class soldiers in charge of rooms could also hand out room duty as a punishment for some offences like being late for roster or dropping ash from a cigarette on the floor. By 5.55am everybody, even those who had reported sick or who wished to see the Company Commander, had to be on parade, sometimes with rifles, most times without for we were not considered competent enough to be in charge of a weapon and ammunition before we had been training for a couple of weeks at least.

When first we did finally parade outside on the parade ground and the NCO called us to 'slope arms', most of the recruits just stood there motionless. But I had spent a few short weeks with the Guards at Caterham and therefore, with a superb Brigade of Guards manner, slapped up my rifle to my shoulder, only to be shouted at by the Sergeant who wanted to know what the Hell I was doing! Then came instruction to everybody on how the Legion rifles were carried and sloped, and how one presented arms to the flag and officers and how one stood to attention for passing NCOs. I was very good at it and drilled and marched well even though the Metropolitan Police Force had not wanted me because, apparently, I had flat feet. I seemed to have very little trouble until one of the Spanish NCOs heard me imitating his very poor French instructions so that whenever he was on duty I knew that I had to watch my step.

I remember vividly two platoon commanders who were in charge of my military instruction at Saïda; Lieutenants Millet and Pepin-Lehalleur, occasionally called *le râleur* (bad-tempered person), who was to become a General later on. They were really fine officers, so typical of the Military Academy of St Cyr which they had both attended. They were men of character, of feeling, of military knowledge and a determination to turn us *bleus* into real légionnaires and not prepared to allow the occasional *salaud* who did not try, to hold back those of us who put our backs into the hard training. Those who did not try soon found that clearing out the *chiottes* (toilets) was much less pleasant than learning about rifles, revolvers and ammunition, and they still had to carry out the duties assigned to others in their free time, and under even closer surveillance by the NCOs.

Here again I must thank all the hard work put in by my French teachers at my *alma mater* for before a very few weeks had passed I was very fluent in the language and understood everything that was shouted at me. Those other Brits, three or four only at the time, who did not share my knowledge of French, found it very difficult to obey orders and eventually found themselves in deep trouble. Not to obey an order for whatever reason, was of course a serious breach of discipline and punishable, first perhaps quite lightly but subsequent disobedience was naturally punished more severely. Confined to barracks was generally accompanied by obligatory duties as part of the *piquet d'incendie* (fire picket) which was usually called out two or three times each evening for practice runs and more of them at weekends.

Salle de Police meant that one carried out normal duties during the day but one slept in barred cells, divested of laces and braces for it was not unknown for delinquents, or those in despair, to hang themselves. In *Salle de Police* offenders were usually awakened several times during the night by the Guard Commander and *reveille* for them was usually about an hour before the usual time so that the barrack square, cells and the guard-room could be swept and tidied. A prison sentence was of course much more serious starting with seven days spent in the prison block, normally built some distance away from the main building and surrounded by ten to twelve feet high walls and with only one entrance. Each punishment, however small, was entered in the personal *livret individual* (Army book).

In Saïda I suppose there were separate cells for a couple of dozen inmates and most of the time I noticed that they must all have been occupied, though I never once entered the precincts as a resident. I did, however, do duty at the entrance of the prison on numerous occasions and saw what happened inside. Those who behaved themselves were escorted by orderlies with bayonets, out into the barrack square for instance, to clean the area, and some even spent some of their punishment in the cookhouse doing the chores. But peeling the spuds and shelling peas and those necessary chores like washing pans and dishes used in the cooking, were also part of the duties of the duty company of the day.

Punishment in the Legion prisons was always hard, but the severity of it all depended on the NCO in charge. Officers paid calls regularly but any complaint of ill-treatment by any inmate only meant more serious reason for complaining later. Some NCOs of prisons were more or less lenient in their treatment of prisoners, but more often than not they were absolute pigs. I suppose that they considered it their job to try their best to persuade their charges to mend their ways and not return to suffer again. The NCOs did not stay forever in charge of a prison and when they came out to normal duties their past work could be taken into consideration by any who had suffered at their hands or not suffered as was sometimes the case.

It was not unknown for ex-prison NCOs to be caught out on dark nights in town and knocked about by ex-prisoners and on one occasion I know for a fact that one particularly demonic German sergeant got in the way of a stray bullet during manoeuvres out in the *bled*. That was during my instruction period at Saïda and no punishment was ever handed out for the culprit was never found. There was no question at that time of prisoners being buried in the desert sand as described by P. C. Wren in one of his romances about the Foreign Legion but I did see them standing, petrified, beside the glaring whitewashed walls, awaiting the word to eat the food that was drying up in the *gamelle* lids in front of them.

In Saïda the days were very hot under the burning desert sun, but the nights were extremely cold. Prisoners did suffer, or so they told me, for as I have previously indicated, I had no personal experience of inside conditions, but we had all joined the Legion, knowing from hearsay that it was not going to be a picnic. I think that my biggest job in those early days, was to make sure that I did not go into prison. I was the perfect soldier; I was sometimes referred to as 'the only Englishman that never tried to escape'. The French that I had learned at grammar school served me well in those early days and I progressed rapidly; the instruction in the use of arms and ammunition, and the drill, came to me readily. Those of my compatriots who did not obey orders because they did not understand the language were constantly assailed with punishments and eventually, in many cases, tried to escape which was stupid for the police were always informed of disappearances after a few hours and they always delighted in returning légionnaires to the barracks. They did not like the Legion, or foreigners; the nomadic Arabs were also ever on the look-out for escapees as there was a price on each head of 300 francs, returned to barracks dead or alive.

At the Instruction Companies, and there were two at Saïda and one at Aïn el Hadjar, further south, there was practically no liberty given for the first month, but then permission was given to visit the town on Sundays and occasionally after 6pm on weekdays. The latter freedom was not often considered as *Reveille* was so early and the training was intense and lasted until 12 noon and lunch. Then there was an obligatory *siesta* when it was an offence to move from the sleeping quarters, until 2.30pm or 3pm when more training was carried out until 5.30pm. We were then fed before more hard work continued. I must mention that the food was not too bad although I do remember that there was never sufficient and the canteen did a roaring trade in *casse-croûtes* (good French-loaf sandwiches) after the evening work was over. Profits from the sales in the canteen were used to supplement the ordinary rations on Feast Days like the French National Day on 14 July, and Camerone Day on 30 April, which marked an infamous Legion battle in Mexico, as well as Christmas Day. Much home-raised pork was eaten and mutton that tasted just like goat because the sheep were bred in the foothills of the Atlas Mountains where there were lots of herbs growing. There was always soup to start off the morning or evening meals and I remember the soup at Saïda best of all for hard tack, ship's biscuit, floated on top of the tureens and our plates and the fact that weevils kept appearing out of them. Rumour had it, and I am quite prepared to believe it, that they were the remains of First World War rations. But we were always hungry and could close our eyes, so eventually we became quite used to the wee sleekit beasties.

As the training continued, more privileges were awarded. If one was not on Fire Picket duty, Guard duty or Patrol duty *en ville,* one could be required to be on duty at one of the three brothels in the village, *La Lune, Le Soleil* or *Le Sphynx.* This was to prevent any disturbances and to see that every soldier got his due and was not taken for a ride so to speak, especially if he had been drinking. These were all officially recognised places where the ladies – French, Spanish and North African – were visited regularly by *le toubib* (military doctor) to ensure they were free from contagious diseases. Standing orders stated that légionnaires visiting these places had to see the duty male nurse at a specially equipped room on the way back from the *bordels* that were all in the Arab quarter. (It would be unheard of to have them anywhere near the residential part). Here they were examined and, prevention being always better than cure, a wash with permanganate of potash was carried out. Records were kept of the names of visitors and with which lady they had lain so that in the event of subsequent illness the lady in question could be examined and put on a blacklist. The fact that a légionnaire had visited the male nurse at the *bureau prophylactique* would save him from punishment should he contract any venereal disease, while others who had failed to do so could expect at least fourteen days confined to barracks for the first offence and a prison sentence thereafter. Picking up a girl in the street, native or European, was cheaper usually, in Africa or Indochina, but infinitely more dangerous.

NCOs made the rounds of these establishments which were considered essential to the well-being of the soldiers, until closing time which was 10pm, although staff, not recruits, might be given passes until midnight or even until daybreak. Rifles were only carried when on guard duty or in times of trouble, and these were not common. Bayonets were worn by men on patrols with the NCO carrying a revolver. Most of the brothel patrols that took place after dark were mainly composed of veterans on the permanent staff who were perhaps more experienced and a number of them were actually married, or *à la colle,* i.e. living together with a woman as man and wife which was occasionally permitted in Algeria and Morocco by the Commanding Officer. In Indochina things were somewhat different as I shall explain later.

But this was some way into our training and I had already learnt some valuable lessons about life in the Legion. Our engagement premium was one thousand francs paid in three instalments. The first instalment of 300 francs was paid after one month, the second after four months and the third after eight months. Our regular pay was one franc a day, which was then worth an English halfpenny, with a packet of dry tobacco each fortnight and a glass of wine with each meal – two on feast days. It must be obvious that this first instalment of 300 francs represented a small fortune and I intended to use it very sparingly. On receiving my fortune, I placed it in my wallet where I kept the few photographs I had brought with me from London to remind me of that Heaven I had left behind. That same evening after dinner I sat on the edge of my bed and was chatting to my newly-made English-speaking friends. A few beds away in the corner was the Corporal in charge of the room who was keeping an eye on us.

First to join me was Cavanagh, the Irishman who had spent time in the English prison, then there came a young seventeen-year-old English lad calling himself Eyton, from Ilford and a Jewish character, probably about twenty-five years old, the son of a very well-known furniture dealer in London and the home counties, a couple of Germans and a Swiss lad. I must say that one could never be sure of the nationality of anybody in the Legion for many gave their nationality as English, German, Swiss or anything else that came into their head at the time of joining. As for Frenchmen, they were actually not allowed to join the Legion under their own correct status for the regular army was of course open to them. Although I suppose that most of them had some deep and secret reason for not wanting the authorities to know who they really were and that was why they were in the Legion under assumed identities.

However, there we were and I was proudly and sentimentally showing off my treasured photographs placing my wallet on the bed by my side while I did so. What a naïve fool I was.

After ten minutes or so of looking at the photographs, the young lad jumped up saying that he must get ready for guard duty and then shortly afterwards the Jewish man said that he must go to the toilet. I put my photos together to put them back in my wallet. The 300 francs were no longer there.

The Irishman with his past history made him the prime suspect. I grabbed him and hauled him over to the Corporal to be searched and held while I dashed off to catch up with the man who had had the most feeble excuse that he was going to the toilets. He was not in the toilets but I did find him back in his room where the look in his eyes told me all I wanted to know. Taking him by the back of the neck I slipped a half-nelson on and said that I would break his neck if he didn't show me where he had hidden my money. It took me some five minutes before he decided to show me, in the presence of four or five of my fellow recruits. We went down to the toilets behind the barracks where a loose brick was taken out to reveal my 300 francs. He lied through his teeth saying that it was not he who had taken the money. He had followed the thief from the room, he said, and had seen where it had been hidden. No proceedings were taken against the culprit though we knew he was lying, but shortly afterwards he was declared 'medically unfit for service with the Legion'. I was not responsible for this as strings were certainly being pulled in England and one day a private plane came to Oran to pick him up to take him home. I do not think that it was a bad thing for him or for the Legion.

The incident had taught me a lesson. Photographs and letters dealing with one's past life before the Legion, or clothing issued by the army, must never be stolen; money and anything else of value that was not considered to be of sentimental value, were always at risk. I found out later that the seventeen-year-old from Ilford had been freed on the grounds that he was well under age and his family wanted him returned. It was about this time that my father informed me that he was in touch with Anthony Eden, the then Foreign Secretary, with a view to having me released, also because of my age, but I wrote to him telling him to forget further action. I had signed my name on a contract for five years with the Legion and the Legion would get those five years.

But back to Saïda and the instruction. Probably the worst job as far as I was concerned was the washing of shirts, underwear and socks, but there were specified times for this *corvée de lavage* and it took place at the *lavabo,* a cement construction under cover with a scrubbing surface on each side of a central yard-deep pit for the cold water into which it seemed water was running at all times. It was just above my waist height and there was enough room for perhaps twenty men at Saïda and in other barracks as well. The same sort of construction, some smaller, some larger, could be seen in those days, but since the invention of launderettes they are disappearing though I suppose that some villages still have their *lavabos* as we have our ancient monuments. There was never any hot water, of course, and soap made by the Legion was used, not the washing powder we know today. Soap was regularly issued to the men. Close by, in the open, was an area with rust-proof wire stretched tightly between cement posts where washing could be hung to dry. Some men did use clothes-pegs but there was always the risk of things being stolen should they be left unguarded. In some places and at certain times a guard, usually someone on light duties, was put on the area during the day. The drying process took very little time during the day, especially during the summer season, because of the intense heat from the sun. Each article of clothing had to be stamped, a laborious, boring job, of one digit at a time, with one's army number – mine was 71824 – to prevent as much pilfering as possible, but it was much safer to watch the washing as it dried, if one had the time to spare.

Quite often the companies under instruction from Saïda or Aïn el Hadjar were ordered to take part in army manoeuvres of considerable scale. Fighting kit in Algeria, in 1937, consisted of *képi* (without the well-known romantic white cover and neck-cover), usual working grey denims, army boots, puttees (only rolled about 6 inches above the top of boots and covering tops of same), heavy dark khaki overcoat with flaps buttoned up to permit freedom of movement for the knees, blue cummerbund (reputed to prevent dysentery), a two-inch belt carrying leather braces, two cartridge pouches containing cartridges, sometimes blanks depending on the seriousness of the operation or manoeuvres, *bidon* (water-bottle), bayonet in sheath, haversack over right shoulder with strap under the belt to keep it firm. The haversack would contain bread and tinned rations for a day, perhaps *singe* (which means monkey, but was actually corned beef) or more sardines or very hard chocolate. The backpack would contain change of underwear, socks, shirts, etc. and would be encircled on three sides by a rolled-up groundsheet which could be joined to others to form a *gitoun* (tent) in case of emergency. On the sides would be an extra pair of *brodequins* (army boots) and a small spade or pick and hoe with handle for digging trenches. The *gamelle* was right on the top as it was usually the thing required most often. The whole would be held in place by leather straps attached to the backpack. Then of course there was the rifle. Scouts would have the old 1916 breech-loading rifle while machine-gun servants would have the lighter, shorter musketoons of a similar period.

Another regular part of our training was completing the *piste d'obstacles*. In the 1980s there was a television programme called the *Krypton Factor* which always reminded me of the obstacle course, which was situated not far from the barracks. Two or three times a week sections spent hours racing in groups up ladders, along ropes, across trenches, under nets, through cement pipes and barbed-wire entanglements, with or without rifles, with punishment handed out to the dilatory. I did not mind the exercise for I was young and very keen. I became a skilled marksman with the badge of *tireur d'élite* and another as *grenadier d'élite* because of my accuracy in hurling grenades thanks to that most British of sports, *le cricket*, that no Frenchman to my knowledge was ever able to comprehend.

My badges were awarded by the Colonel of the regiment but carried no real privileges; they were, however, an indication to my future commanders of my best position in combat. Groups were set against each other to find the fittest and fastest in the company and extra glasses of wine, or extra leave in town would be granted to the winners. On special occasions the *piste* would end with a rifle shooting contest and competitive throwing of unarmed grenades at various distances which made the occasion much more interesting, probably because I was so good at it.

As I was quite tall, nearly six foot, and very smart where drill was concerned, I could easily be placed in the front rank whence I could lead the singing when we were out marching *sans cadence.* I soon learned Legion songs which were often enough quite bawdy, but very often I would sing English marching songs of the First World War and the others soon picked them up, or at least the tunes. The Germans had so many good marching songs and felt it essential for their Fatherland to try and out-sing me. The Italians were also part of the game and, although they did not have so many songs for marching, they very soon sang romantic numbers adapting them to the rhythm of the march. It was all good clean fun and served its purpose for the officers who trained us, and led us, were convinced of the importance of the singing to keep up our spirits after a long hard day or part of the day in the quasi-desert and to let the natives know that we were there, ready to spring into action should the occasion arise. The French, German and Italian songs I sang then, I sing still today and the tunes will remain with me forever. Some of the words will not.

I remember at Saïda there was a very big American called Nichols who played the tuba in the small music detachment that was used to render honours to visiting personalities, military and civic, to supply *clairons* to sound *Reveille, soupe, courier, extinction des feux* etc. and to play our training companies back into the barracks after lengthy route marches. This is a very important task for when soldiers are at their lowest after traipsing for hours over stony, sandy wastelands, or through deep, muddy rice fields, as I found out later, nothing makes them lift their heads higher and march with renewed energy and pride than the sound of the *clique* composed of trumpets, fifes and kettle-drums, or even the complete military band with saxophones, trombones, tubas, basses, bassoons and big drum besides the *clique* when attached to the main barracks like Sidi-bel-Abbès, Fès, Meknès and Vietri in those far-off days. The American had been in the Legion at Saïda for some sixteen years and I do not think he had ever paid for a drink in all that time for he was a great story-teller, and for a beer or two he would go on for hours. I did not see much of him myself, but because he was, shall we say English-speaking, and a bit of a character, he was very well known.

During training we were called upon to march long distances, perhaps ten miles in the morning and five more during the afternoon, two or three times a week, gradually increasing until we were doing fifteen miles and twelve miles by which time the slackers or those with foot or other disorders had been discovered and thrown out or given jobs in the infirmary, canteen or kitchen. I found I marched well and gradually got to enjoy the marches out in the parched and dusty countryside. The recognised rate was 4km per fifty minutes when on long marches, then a ten-minute break to snatch a quick smoke, a quick drink or a rapid sandwich. There were men who could never resist filling their *bidons* (tin water-bottles covered with cloth which, if kept damp, ensured that the contents remained reasonably cool) with wine instead of water, but the NCOs, having done the same thing themselves before promotion, kept their eyes on men suspected of doing it for it was very much against regulations. If they caught anybody it meant not only punishment on returning to barracks but the offender was forced to empty the wine out and go without a drink for the rest of the march, an awful punishment in itself. Companions who offered their water to the offender were also severely punished. These marches did sort out the real men from the chaff; those who could not keep up were left behind to make their own way home, but I must admit that stragglers were very rare. The parade march was at a slower speed, eighty-eight paces to the minute, though I never did get around to counting them, perhaps very slightly quicker than the funereal slow march of the Brigade of Guards that I had once known. But it must be understood that the Legion marches were so often on sandy ground which is not the best thing to walk on. A small point here, and my article about it was published a few months ago in *Letters to the Editor* (*Daily Telegraph*), is that I found out the best way to prevent blisters on the feet was to adopt the *chaussettes Russes* method of not using socks but to lay each foot on a clean piece of linen such as a bit of an old shirt, and wrap the ends around the foot before placing it in the boot. The bits of shirt that showed above the boot were covered by the *bands molletières* (puttees). I always found it most efficacious.

Some poor individuals were not cut out for military life. I took to it like a duck to water, but they should have gone into banking or teaching for they were not going to have a happy life in the Foreign Legion. NCOs, for the most part, concentrated on these unfortunate characters and occasionally forgot about the capable ones, so we did profit by their presence and the truth of the saying that the Devil takes the hindmost I soon learned during instruction, though I and others like me were nearly always ready to help when it suited our purpose and time was available. One offender could easily bring group punishment but it was usually just a few turns around the barrack square which was perhaps a good half-mile round, in full marching kit weighing thirty pounds or more depending on the NCO inflicting the punishment, but it would be after the evening meal which was definitely not good. The miscreant causing the extra slogging was never popular with his colleagues.

Regularly, once a month during training at Saïda, manoeuvres were carried out about ten miles or so from the barracks, in the *bled* as the stony desert was called, when live ammunition was used. Every cartridge was counted and unused rounds collected under the wary eye of an NCO, just to prevent 'accidents' happening afterwards.

Evenings were spent cleaning rifles and equipment until 21.00h which just allowed time for a drink and a snack, funds permitting, at the *Foyer* before rollcall at 22.00h.

✹

It was quite obvious by the continuous exercises and manoeuvres undertaken by the Legion and the other troops in the area, the Colonial Regiments, the Spahis, and the native Tirailleurs who had mainly French officers and NCOs, that there was great unease in North Africa during those years just before the Second World War came. But there was also unease amongst the different nationalities within the Legion. The beliefs and characters of these men who could be nameless, could not be so easily hidden from others. Many Jews had joined the Legion about that time as they fled from Nazi oppression in Europe and for the most part they were definitely not into drill, marching, manoeuvres or hard manual work and they suffered. They had joined up for the 'duration of the war' which was a special category arranged particularly for them and for which I suppose they were expected to be grateful to France. But how they suffered! There seemed to be no real reason for it except for the fact they were Jews. There was only very rarely a synagogue in the vicinity of Legion barracks and no regulation to permit them to worship according to their faith, though it would have surprised me to find that many of them were actually practising Jews. As I have intimated, they were, on the whole, poor soldiers, and it didn't help that 60 per cent of the Legion was German in those days. NCOs treated them with derision and scorn but they seemed to accept their destiny; at least in the Legion they were still alive while millions of their fellows were being persecuted and massacred in Germany, Poland, Russia and Eastern Europe. But even everyday Legion life was a compromise for these poor people. Légionnaires were pig-breeders *par excellence* and pork was very often on the menu, as was the famous black pudding. A good friend once asked me what the Jews ate while we enjoyed our pork which is forbidden them. It was a very good question to which I might one of these days find an answer. My friend's mother was quite sure that when faced with the inevitable, when there was no choice at all, a non-practising Jew would be allowed to succumb, and as I had never noticed any variation of menu in the Legion to accommodate racial requirements, I suppose that was the answer.

There was really no time for making friends at Saïda, well not for me anyhow. I found many of the German recruits were arrogant bullies, conscious of the fact that they were more numerous than any other nationality and they stuck together. Argue with one and there were a dozen or more who immediately wanted to take part in the argument and there was only one side to an argument – the German one.

There were also lots of Spaniards who had fled from Spain and the Fascist domination after the Civil War there and they appealed to me almost as much as the Germans for they also stuck together; they were very untidy into the bargain and untidiness did not just reflect on those that were but could cause all sorts of trouble to members of the rooms where they were quartered and to the particular groups or sections to which they belonged militarily.

Punishment was usually meted out to groups as well as to the individuals causing the trouble so there was almost continuous conflict during instruction, but I kept myself to myself as much as possible and was considered by the majority as a real English diplomat, an arbiter called upon pretty often to settle disputes.

It was very close to the end of our instruction when we were called to fall in on the parade ground one evening and told to get into marching kit, then issued with our rifles and five cartridges each. The time was 23.00h and by midnight we were led off by Lt Pepin-Lehalleur. We numbered just under a hundred men – three sections each commanded by a Lieutenant and comprising three groups of a Sergeant, a Corporal or Lance-Corporal, two scouts, a light machine-gun with gunner and loader, and three riflemen.

As usual we knew not the why nor the wherefore. We just marched and marched and marched through the night with only the briefest rests and intervals. Next morning, we stopped for half an hour or so to eat the bread and chocolate with which we had been issued before departure. We were also told that the mobile kitchen was following and we would eventually have a real meal. That was all we were told. As usual during any sortie that we made from Saïda, we were followed by a couple of Arabs, we called them *schleux* which was not very complimentary, with donkeys laden with *casse-croûtes* and there were always *baguettes*, various sausages and of course the famous *boudin* again, the staple diet of the Legion; the black pudding. In fact the March of the French Foreign Legion is called *Le Boudin* and is sung whenever and wherever Légionnaires, or ex-Légionnaires congregate:

Tiens, voilà du boudin, voilà du boudin, voilà du boudin,
Pour les Alsaciens, les Suisses et les Lorrains...

Pour les Belges il n'y en a plus, pour les Belges il n'y en a plus,
Ce sont les tireurs au cul....
Pour les Belges il n'y en a plus...ce sont les tireurs au cul...!

Rough translation:

Here we have black pudding...
For men from Alsace, from Switzerland and Lorraine...
But there isn't any for the Belgians... for they are the greatest crawlers...!

Besides beer and lemonade in bottles, one could also purchase cigarettes, small cigars, matches and so on but the most surprising fact about the business was that the vendors to my knowledge were never told that we were going out, but they were always there. In fact, very often they were wherever we were going before us and we were, had we any money, always very grateful for their presence. I suppose that they had been selling to légionnaires doing instruction at Saïda for so many years that they knew every move that was made. There was not much difference between the prices the Arabs charged and the prices we had to pay in town, though we always tried to beat them down.

It must have been three o'clock in the afternoon when we arrived at our destination, a small village surrounded by palm trees with a well in the middle. The Lieutenant and our section of thirty men under Lt Pepin-Lehalleur entered the village having fired several rounds into the air as a warning. The *Caids,* the local chieftains, realising that we were in force, advanced towards us with their hands in the air and fell on their knees with bowed heads as we approached. The other inhabitants clustered together at the end of the village looking about as dangerous as new-born babes. Shortly afterwards we saw coming towards us from the opposite direction, a number of covered lorries laden with French Colonial troops and within half an hour or so, a Major had taken command of the situation and the *Caïds,* four of them, had been handcuffed and thrown into one of the lorries. After a few words between the Major and our officers, the whole convoy of Colonial troops turned and departed whence they had come. We left in the direction of Saïda meeting up shortly afterwards with the mobile kitchen. A halt was called, we were fed and within the hour we were again on our way back to barracks. Word got out the next day that two Frenchmen had been murdered and the village and the *Caïds* in particular were held responsible so they had to be taken back to Tiaret, the departmental main town, for trial.

Our training company at Saïda had been the closest detachment of 'shock troops' to the village in question so that was why, as our training was almost at an end, we had been sent. The Legion could always be relied upon to be ready for trouble before any other troop. The next Regimental Bulletin that came out carried the Colonel's congratulations on a job well done and a few days later we came to the end of our thirteen weeks training. We were ready for integration into the real regiments of the Legion and for our new future.

5
The Legion, La Musique and L'amour

O n completion of our instruction at Saïda, we re-joined the *Compagnie de Passage* at Sidi-bel-Abbès from where we had set out three months before, feeling that we were now real légionnaires and that real Legion life was about to begin. We were eager to see some of those exciting places we had heard about. We would be transferred to one of the regiments far from Algeria: the 2nd stationed at Meknès, the 3rd at Fès or the 4th at Marrakech – all in Morocco – or the 6th Regiment in the Levant (Middle East) or even the 5th out in Indochina. They all had outposts where garrison spit and polish rules and regulations were to all intents and purposes quite forgotten, or so we had been told.

Whilst others did indeed get posted to those places (and later I was to hear from them that rules, regulations and discipline were more sternly enforced in the outposts than in the larger depots and the novelty and glamour soon wore off) there was a big surprise in store, and a very disappointing one at the time, for me. At an interview in the *compagnie de passage No. 1* (the company office), I happened to mention that I had strummed the mandolin a bit at evening sing-songs at home and this was immediately taken up by the Captain who said that the Music of the Regiment was looking for volunteers and I had just volunteered. Within hours I was transferred to Quartier Vienot to a huge four-storey block which housed the *Musique*. This was located just across the road from the *compagnie!* I was interviewed by Monsieur Petit, the *Sous-Chef* or Deputy Chief of the Music who produced a mandolin and told me to perform. It was a very poor show that I put on for I did not want my dreams of oases in the desert to be stolen from me. After all, I had come to the Legion for adventure and I had not seen very much of it so far. But M. Petit had other ideas in store for me. I would be ideal for the office of the Regimental Music for did I not have an excellent education behind me? I was smart in appearance and correct in my attitude and I was just what they wanted in the bureau. I could also learn to play the tenor saxophone when I was not wanted in the office. My French was excellent by this time although it did still cause some amusement on occasions.

So it was that I joined the Regimental Music and although it was not what I had wanted, it certainly wasn't a hard life and I actually began to enjoy it. At that time in the office there was a Lance-Sergeant called Vilaers and a first-class musician called Jean Vandam. The former was French but had joined the Legion by stating he was of Swiss origin. I am quite sure that he was of excellent family but had blotted his copybook somewhere at some time and like so many, found refuge in anonymity in the Legion. The latter was Belgian with a wonderful baritone voice quite befitting the first prize winner of the Namur Conservatory which he was. We made a good team and got on very well together.

Vandam was having an affair with a beautiful French girl who worked in the Post Office in Bel-Abbès. She was much younger than he and her mother with whom she lived, was very much against the affair, but they did seem to be very much in love with each other. It was a very strange business on which I pondered long hours without discovering how such a lovely twenty-year-old girl, who was quite well off, could possibly have such a visible love for a 1st class musician of the Legion with a past veiled in mystery, no prospects, and who bore a fair resemblance to the very unattractive, though *sympathique* famous French film star, Fernandel. They were still seeing each other as often as possible in May 1941 when I left for Morocco and then the Far East and I often wonder what became of them. Vilaers was a loner who, although most enjoyable company inside, rarely went out. He read a lot and was quite a philosopher. But perhaps it was his air of mystery which made him so attractive. As I spent more time in the Legion, I learnt that we légionnaires certainly had an appeal to the local ladies.

We had some wonderful evenings in the office and life became very comfortable. At the end of the day, particularly in winter, M. Petit would tell me to go into town and buy bread and *saindoux*. *Saindoux* is reduced lard, beautifully white in colour and I loved it. Were I able to find it in Bath I am afraid all the dietary instructions from my doctor and my wife would go by the board! M. Petit would then produce a couple of bottles of red wine which, with a few cloves, a couple of sliced oranges, a lemon and plenty of sugar, would be heated on the cast-iron stove we had in the middle of the office. We would spend the rest of the evening telling of things that had happened in our various lives. My accent used to make them laugh a lot during the first few months but gradually, as my proficiency advanced, they found they could not really fault me.

But I must tell about one occasion in the early days in the *Musique* when I had been sent to buy some tins of tripe at the food store in town. It was owned by a Mr and Mrs Gomez who were, as the name suggests, one of the many Spanish families in Algeria at that time and they employed about a dozen young ladies, all of whom spoke French and Spanish. I had been there often to buy food but had never bought tripe before. M. Petit had explained that he wanted *tripes à la mode de Caen* on this occasion rather than *saindoux*. I duly asked one of the young ladies for two tins of the required tripe. I was amazed at the response for the whole store seemed to burst out laughing. The young lady asked me to repeat what I had said and again there were howls of laughter till Madame Gomez intervened and brought the normal, serious atmosphere back to the store and ordered the girl to bring me my two tins of tripe. I paid and left, feeling puzzled. Returning to the office I explained what had happened to M. Petit and my friends and they, between guffaws, explained that my pronunciation of the word *Caen* was very similar to the word describing a certain very private part of the female anatomy! It took me a very long time to live the story down and for many months afterwards I blushed each time I went into the Gomez store while the young ladies smiled precociously. I practised the pronunciation of the word *Caen* for weeks on end and never made the same mistake again.

The office staff were great characters and I soon found that M. Petit was also a super person with a lovely wife and five or six children. The Petit family, not really *petite* was it? lived just across the road from the barracks in military quarters and must have found it rather small accommodation for the size of the family. Joseph, a 2nd class musician, originally from Lorraine, had been M. Petit's *ordonnance* or orderly (a military home-help) for a number of years and seemed to enjoy cleaning the house instead of playing the tuba in the orchestra. So there I was, whether I liked it or not, a member of the famous *Musique* of the 1st Regiment of the Foreign Legion, producing the finest Military Music of France. I decided to make the best of it.

The Regimental Music in any army seems to receive special privileges like the Bands of the Royal Marines in Britain, the Metropolitan Police, the Hussars, the Horse Guards and the Royal Air Force which all frequently grace our Royal processions. It is also true of the Band of the French Foreign Legion. They miss most of the manoeuvres and guard duties but have to spend a lot of time practising. From the very start of the Legion in 1831, there were twenty-six members of the Music and by 1845 there were at least fifty in each of the two regiments of the Legion. It is not surprising when one considers that ever since those early days there have been many German, Viennese, Polish and Hungarian légionnaires recognised as musicians in renowned orchestras in their native lands, who entered the ranks of the Legion. In the past, they had found many reasons for leaving their homeland but in my time, they were fleeing the Nazi boot for most of them were Jews, while others disagreed with Nazi policy.

The Musics of the 1st, 2nd, 3rd, 4th, 5th, and 6th Regiments of my day were all capable of excellent performances of classical oeuvres by the great masters to delight audiences in their particular territories. Each regiment also had its *clique* or bugle and drum band with its fifes, according to some sources only used nowadays in the Legion. In 1937, I discovered the great composers via the superb orchestra of the 1st Regiment at Sidi-bel-Abbès under the direction of Captain Aka and it was an appreciation which would last a lifetime. Several years later, Beryl and I were most fortunate when holidaying in Venice to happen upon the funeral of Stravinsky and were able to enter the church and take photographs. It was a most moving occasion carried out in the true Venetian manner with funereal gondolas transporting the coffin decorated in purple, black and silver. The power of music will never diminish.

The Legion took music seriously and knew its importance. So much so that on one occasion, gramophone recordings were to be made of the Legion orchestra and the experts came along to manage the whole proceedings. What a business it was. The recordings were to be made in the *Salle de Répétition* which, the experts deemed, was found wanting in the quality of its acoustics and so the whole room had to be hung with regulation blankets, on the walls and on the ceiling and a carpet had to go on the floor. The recording instruments were placed in Captain Aka's office and notices were hung all over the place threatening severe punishment should any noise be heard when the red light was on, indicating that recording was in progress. It took weeks to get to the final stage and a limited number of classical records were made. During one final recording of L'Arlésienne, one of *le Père Aka's* favourites, he detected a false note from the woodwind section that would probably have gone unnoticed to all but the most critical ear. He had forgotten where he was and what he was doing and came out with the most wonderful descriptions of the parentage of the offender. The whole piece had to be repeated, of course, but he kept the original and we listened to it, and laughed with him about it, for many months afterwards.

Taking an important part in the recordings as soloist, was my friend Burin, a great violinist of Russian-Jewish birth who could make even the toughest of us weep to the sound of his instrument as he played rhapsodies or *morceaux choisis* learned by heart during his childhood. All the suffering of the Jewish race seemed to be stored with that man and his violin and which he allowed to come out to charm all who listened. The trouble with Burin (he told me one day that his real name was Ginsberg) was that he liked Scotch, and he liked brandy, and he adored cigars, and they were very expensive. He used to run up a huge bill at one or other of the better restaurants in town and would not pay until the Manager got in touch with the Colonel of the Regiment and the money was stopped from his pay (he was a Lance-Sergeant). Meanwhile several times a month he would come back to barracks absolutely *blotto* and would be given a prison sentence, particularly severe should he be absent from a concert.

Most NCOs of the prisons at that time were German, and they, like their Nazi fellows, did not like the Jews and when Burin went inside it was never going to be a picnic. He spent most of his time there breaking up boulders into smaller rocks and then into smaller stones and then into pebbles for making roads and footpaths, using a variety of hammers in the process, none of them helping very much to keep his hands in good condition for his violin playing. When the Sergeant tired of this sport, Burin would have to put his haversack on his back. It would be filled with some of the rocks he himself had broken up and instead of the usual leather straps there would be bare wire to hold the pack on his back. He would then have to double round the prison compound until he dropped when a bucket of water would be thrown over him by one of the other inmates, to get him under way again, and again and again. This was certainly not done to make him decide to mend his ways, but just unadulterated torture for torture's sake and for being a Jew. It would take Burin's friends many weeks of treatment with ointments to his hands before he could play again after a spell in prison, although the Colonel would authorise his coming out to play in concerts, not as a soloist of course, but as part of the orchestra when the *Chef de Musique* requested it. Then, a few months after coming out of prison he would be back in again. I often thought that Burin had taken on his own poor thin shoulders all the trouble and strife of all the Jews of the world.

Captain Aka retired in 1939 to take over as Head of the Music of the Peugeot factory at Montbéliard in south-western France. He was replaced by Captain Bria who came from a Colonial Regiment and was also a brilliant musician, but he could never command the great love and respect that his predecessor had received from his musicians.

One of my duties was to take Captain Bria's lunch-time meal to him at his home which he shared with his family. I would cycle out to their apartment which was on the third floor of an imposing apartment block, half a mile from the barracks. Madame Bria was always very interested in me and my past and wondered what I was doing there. She was quite beautiful in a Spanish *duenna* sort of way and she loved her food; on at least two occasions I was invited to lunch to partake of her personally-prepared favourite, *l'aïoli*, a dish probably originating in or near Marseilles being primarily mayonnaise with crushed garlic and used as a dip. At the time I disliked garlic intensely, particularly because it was so antisocial, but I felt I had to bear with it as Madame Bria set such great store by it. I have since changed my opinion and enjoy it often; not only is it delicious but it has been proven to have many therapeutic qualities.

One of my main responsibilities in the office of the famous *Musique* was to type out and print on a *Cyclostyle* machine, two hundred copies of the programme for the next concert and then distribute them throughout the town. I had to type the programme out on a special carbon paper which was laid on a gel contained in a tin tray. When the paper was removed the typed words remained on the gel, in reverse. The blank space on the programme was then pressed on to the gel and the blue letters appeared on the programme. It was a boring process and I was not always successful. Typing errors meant a repetition of the whole process which meant even more time and effort.

I also had to ensure that there was sufficient liquid polish for the brass instruments. The musicians did their own polishing but I made the polish from 'Fuller's Earth' and turpentine, two products that I obtained from the small, very old-fashioned, *droguerie* owned by M. Mira who was assisted by his lovely daughter, Elvira. On the death of her father in 1939, Elvira took over the shop herself. At this shop one could buy essences of perfumes, herbs, pure alcohol, soaps etc – a real drug shop. Elvira had a disabled mother at home so she didn't really have a most enjoyable, free life. The family were of Spanish descent so Elvira could never go out on her own which rather restricted any courtships. However, I found I was attracted to Elvira and she seemed to like me and so we did step out for a short while. She had a brother who was married and worked in one of the banks in the town and he and I got on well enough. But he was protective of his sister and made it very clear that the family would expect Elvira to marry a member of the Catholic faith. At that time, I did not consider myself to be a Catholic although I had been baptised at the Catholic church in Burnopfield, County Durham. I had been a member of the Scouts at Tanfield which was affiliated to the Church of England and therefore I had never considered myself to be anything other than a member of the Anglican church. In fact, at Grammar School I always stayed in my seat when the first lesson, always religious studies, began and the Catholics, and one Atheist I remember, left the classroom to wait in the corridor. Elvira and I remained good friends, that's all, and I hope I provided her with some light diversion from everyday life, as she did for me. I suppose I could regret the lack of physical intimacy with Elvira, but I am proud of my behaviour: I was English and feel that I behaved like a gentleman, as it was expected of me, although the opportunities to misbehave were undoubtedly there.

I had been issued with my bicycle not only to take lunch to the captain but also to deliver programmes in town and to tout for clients to advertise in our programmes and so obtain support for our funds. Concerts were given each Sunday and on Feast days at the bandstand opposite the Theatre on the *Place du Théâtre*, a quite large cemented square in the middle of the town, surrounded by palm trees which gave a certain amount of shade. Concerts usually began at 5pm.

There were numerous metal benches placed round the bandstand and they were very popular with young courting and even married couples taking their afternoon or evening promenades. Several bars of the vicinity also had tables on the cement and drinks were served. It was my job to distribute the programmes that I had produced and then, when there were empty seats on the bandstand because musicians were ill or had failed to turn up (which would mean severe punishment for the offender), I would get out my saxophone, that I always took along just in case, and take my place with the orchestra.

In 1939, for the French National Day on 14th July, just weeks before the outbreak of war, the *Musique*, for the first time ever, went to Paris to lead the parade down the Champs Elysées. We were dressed smartly as befitted the occasion, in white *képis*, blue cummerbunds and *épaulettes*. We stayed for four days and on the last evening, just in front of the Bastille where the French Revolution began in 1793, I danced for a while with Marlene Dietrich. Our goodbye kiss was really quite something and I will never forget it. I flatter myself, but Marlene once starred with Gary Cooper in a film about the Legion and I often wonder whether, when she filmed it, she remembered me.

Shortly before the Second World War broke out in 1939, Jock Lawrence, a trombonist, came to the end of his engagement and was repatriated to Britain. I presume that he must have been the stranger who called on my brother Joe in Acton, London, in a rather poor condition though I have never heard of him since. I remember wondering at the time why Jock would be leaving, for life was pretty good in the *Musique* and he did not seem to have any problems. What happened to Jock? He would certainly be called up when war broke out, unless he managed to find himself a 'soft number'.

Besides Jock, a Scotsman of course, who also played the violin in the orchestra, and myself, were Jules Dardenne, a Belgian of very good background in his native country who played the trumpet and Théodor Ulrich from Estonia who played the violin and bass saxophone. We were known as the Four Musketeers and spoke English together, used the same bistros and spent much of our spare time in each other's company. At that time, I was practically teetotal and never drank the wine issued at mealtimes. I used to exchange it alternately with my grateful friends for their ration of dessert. The main point of having a group of close friends was really for protection, as often enough single soldiers would be found lying dead or badly beaten up in the back streets having been attacked by other soldiers or Arab gangs.

It was not only at the hands of the Arabs, or even other soldiers, that men died, for I remember that one of my friends in the *Musique,* named Vandevelde, another Belgian, who played the violoncello very well indeed, committed suicide. That was the final decision at the enquiry, but did he just fall, or was he pushed? He did drink quite a lot and was very outspoken as far as the Germans were concerned for he did not like them at all. I was one of the first on the scene, not because any shout or commotion was heard, but because I just happened to be on my way out and was on the stairs when the unfortunate incident took place. Halfway down the only flight of stairs that led from the office to the ground floor where I parked my bicycle, I saw something big drop down past me, into the stairwell, and then heard a dull thump. I hurried down and there was my friend, stretched out with his knees up to his chin, with his head at a strange angle. I tried to find a beat at his throat without success, got the shining top of the bell off my bike and held it to his mouth, but there no sign of life. I stayed with him, tears in my eyes, for as yet I had not encountered the violent deaths that I was to discover later in Indochina, until someone fetched an *infirmier* and declared him dead. What a sad loss, and no reason for it was ever found, or at least made public, for that was Legion practice.

Jock Lawrence had been giving English lessons to quite a number of young lads and lasses, all in their teens, and when he left he passed them all on to me so I had quite the little business going. My job in the office permitted all sorts of freedom though it did cost me a number of evening meals to recompense my colleagues when they did duty for me. By this time, I was twenty-one and quite popular with the young ladies of sixteen or seventeen who were studying English for their *baccalauréat*. There were also young men who wanted English lessons, of course, but they were altogether more serious in their studies. One or two of them were even related to Algerian or Moroccan ruling families and destined for high office. The families of my pupils were always very friendly and courteous to le *petit anglais* as they called me (by *petit* they did not mean 'small' but 'genteel', or so I was told). They trusted me to behave correctly with their daughters but it was often very difficult indeed, for most of them were very attractive and sometimes very precocious.

There was the Chenillot family that I remember particularly well, consisting of mother and father, a son and a daughter, Lucienne. Odile, from Alsace-Lorraine, was the elderly family retainer. Lucienne was probably my best pupil. She was tall, well developed, attractive and pleasant with a lovely sense of humour. Her parents were in charge of one of the larger schools of the town and Monsieur was also a Major of the Reserve Army. When I was not on duty, I was invited to meals by Madame Chenillot and I always enjoyed the company. With hindsight, I realise that the family were hoping that a serious relationship would develop between Lucienne and myself, for the young lady had apparently fallen in love with me. For me, however, it was very much a platonic friendship as, at that time in my life, I had absolutely no intention of tying myself down.

When the General Mobilisation came in France I was issued with a rifle and ammunition, but was still allowed as much freedom as before, thanks to a special pass signed by the Commanding Officer of the Regiment, Colonel Azan, who had always been kind and considerate to me. He seemed to treat me as a special case – again on account of my being English – and would always stop and talk when we met.

But there were times that being English did not work in my favour and relations between nations on the international stage could not fail to permeate down to a very local and personal level. On 4th July 1940, for example, as I was walking through the market on my way to the bar for my usual rum and blackcurrant, I saw Madame Chenillot approaching. Normally she would have stopped and chatted for a while. I raised my *képi* and said *bonjour*, but she turned her head and marched on. I turned and gazed after her wondering why on earth she had snubbed me. After a few yards, I saw her turn and come back towards me, "Monsieur Murray," she said drily, "after what happened at Oran this morning, please do not ever speak to me again." I forgot about my drink and went to buy a newspaper. There in great bold headlines the paper told of how a good part of the French fleet, because of a Franco-German agreement, had taken refuge in the naval base of Mers-el-Kébir. After fruitless negotiations, and so that the vessels would not fall into German hands, the British had sunk and damaged many of them. One battleship and two destroyers escaped to Toulon but the rest of the French fleet was put out of action by the British guns. 1,300 French seamen died. No wonder that Mme Chenillot was in despair and the French nation filled with hate for many months afterwards.

It was indeed a sorry affair. I was disappointed by Madame's attitude for how was I to blame?

Opinions seemed to differ as to the reasons for the incident, but most of them appeared to condemn Churchill for being too hasty in his orders. The Germans were in control in France and both Darlan and Pétain, in an unenviable position, were conscious of the danger to France should they go against the Nazi wishes. Earlier in 1940, on 28th March 1940, the French had guaranteed Britain that there would never be a separate armistice and Admiral Darlan had told Churchill on 11th June that, in the event of an armistice, he would order all French ships to sail to British-held ports. On 16th June, Lord Halifax sent telegrams to the French Government stating that Britain would agree to a separate armistice for France in those conditions. Then Britain, or to be precise, Churchill, made a most dramatic offer of union with France. Pétain refused to order the fleet to sail as requested but added that the ships would not be surrendered and Darlan honoured his promise to Churchill by ordering French ships to be scuttled should the Germans attempt to take them. However, under the terms of the Armistice, units of the French fleet could also sail to German or Italian ports to be demobilised. But Churchill trusted neither Germans, Italians nor Pétain and considered that the last option held a possible loophole for the enemy and the fate of democracy was in his hands. He told me later when I was his bodyguard and we talked about the Legion, the French and Oran, that it was a command he had always regretted, not because it was wrong, but because so many men had to perish and so many French ships had to be destroyed when they could so easily have been used by the Allies to defeat the Axis forces. As in most cases, Churchill, I found, could always discover reasons for his actions that leaned in his favour, and who am I to criticise, he did win in the end. However, back to 1940 and needless to say, my lessons with Lucienne ceased forthwith.

A week later I was walking down the boulevard just in front of the Continental Hotel when I spotted Major Chenillot coming towards me. He was in uniform so I brought up my hand to the brim of my *képi* in a smashing salute. He replied to my salute correctly, but also stretched out his hand in the familiar way among friends and asked me how it was that they no longer saw me at his home. I did not wish to implicate his wife, so I told him that I had thought that it might be embarrassing after Mers-el-Kébir. He asked me if I was free that evening and if so I must come along for dinner otherwise he would have to have a word with my new Colonel, Robert. I duly went along that evening to give the usual lesson to Lucienne, who seemed very relieved to see me again. Madame had put on a delicious meal and everything carried on as if nothing had happened. We were back to normal and I was very pleased.

Early in 1941, I went to say goodbye to these good friends. I was leaving the very next day for Casablanca to sail to the Far East. After dinner, I kissed the members of the family except Lucienne who was told by her mother to accompany me to the door. She dropped a letter that she had held in her hand; we both automatically bent down to pick it up and as we straightened our backs on rising our lips met in our first kiss. That was that.

She handed me the letter and I carried it with me for many years afterwards. I remember it so well, word for precious word. It was in French of course: "Monsieur Murray, know that from the very first day a silly young girl was in love with you...that she struggled desperately against sentiments that could never be reciprocated...but do not worry, dear Mr Murray, I love life too much to play the Juliet of your beloved Shakespeare...leave if you wish but know that you are taking my heart with you, forever...Adieu!"

Eventually, when the British forces arrived in North Africa she married a Polish pilot in the RAF and had a child. But, her mother told me many years later, he was a bit of a bounder and they divorced. She then married a Doctor of Letters and we met once in Belfort where they lived. She appeared to be quite happy although she did seem to regard me with a certain amount of unforgiving disdain.

Another interesting character living in Sidi-bel-Abbès at the time was a very eccentric so-called Scandinavian lady who lived near the Arab quarters in a rambling cement bungalow with her aged mother. They spoke perfect English and the daughter went under the name of Neilson. I decided she was British-born, married at some time to a Scandinavian. She kept a goodly collection of stray cats and dogs and even began to collect a selection of stray légionnaires, inviting them to meals. She spoke several languages and used to go around in quasi-Arab dress but without *yashmak*. This was just before war broke out and I was called into the office of the *2me. Bureau* where the Intelligence Officer, Corporal Vasseur, asked me to find out anything I could about the ladies and keep an eye on them. I was to report regularly to him. I never did find out anything suspicious about the ladies but I've always had a faint suspicion that the daughter was up to no good and her mother just a front. I was never able to discover any written material nor any method of communication with the outside world other than the usual postal service which was, I am sure, censored at the time. But it goes to show that even before war was officially declared, tensions were beginning to run high.

Hélène Eruimy, another pupil, was quite lovely in a Jewish sort of way, but without much colour and spent most of her time studying very hard. She had a most exciting figure, with everything in the right place, and plenty of it! But she was not interested in her English teacher as a romantic pastime, even though her younger sister took great delight in teasing us both about a possible union.

Then there was the lovely Claudine Piat. Her parents were headteachers at a school on the outskirts of town and were always very friendly. Claudine's brother was eventually to go to the St. Maixent Military Academy and he wrote to me. My reply must have gone astray for he never replied and it was unusual, I have since found, to sever friendships forged during time in the Legion.

There was also the Sanañes family who for many years had been the main furniture dealers in the town in the *Boulevard de la République*. One of the sons and a daughter, Lydia, were among my pupils. They both worked very hard but they would never have been the best linguists in the world. Still, they managed to get through their exams and many years later Lydia married one of my *Musique* colleagues, Hermann Lohr, who played the euphonium and cello. He used to give Lydia German lessons and when last I heard of them, they were living in New York. The family were Jewish and I was always served coffee and Jewish cakes for which Madame Sanañes was well known.

My favourite bar in Sidi-bel-Abbès at the time was the Bar de la Légion, just a few hundred yards from the barracks and here I made friends with another Madame Sanañes and her two daughters, Marguerite, a bright Spanish-looking nineteen-year-old, and Berthe, a serious, lovely girl of twenty-one. It was a perfect haven from the martial atmosphere of the barracks. They were often visited by a cousin from Mascara, a wine-making town some sixty miles to the east, where her father was Mayor. Renée was beautiful and she knew it. She was the same age as Berthe, but always under the watchful eye of her aunt. Nevertheless, we enjoyed each other's company and managed to meet in the cinema on occasions, though we never entered or left the building together. It was most frustrating, but also rather exciting. When I returned to England in 1946 I wrote to Renée and even proposed to her. Proxy marriages were still permitted then – a leftover from the war years – and she replied that she was in favour of the engagement but that she would like to visit England before making up her mind. I sent her a diamond engagement ring and £100 to help her decide, asking her to meet me in Marseilles on a certain day. It was all hopelessly romantic; the stuff of films. It is probably not surprising that I never heard from Renée ever again. But I was young and did not take the rejection to heart, not for long anyway.

Another job that fell to me as soon as I was in the Music, was to act as guide and entertainer to visiting personalities who spoke English, a decision conveyed to me by the Regimental Sergeant-Major in charge of the *Service Général* who was responsible for the general maintenance of the barracks. There was a theatre in Sidi-bel-Abbès, and two European cinemas so visits were often made by famous people on tour. They always wanted to visit the Legion barracks, museum and *Salle d'Honneur*. This became part of my job and I soon achieved a reputation as a well-informed guide. British and RAF Officers and men from ships anchored in Oran, Arzew or Mers-el-Kébir were frequent visitors as well as a surprising number of high-profile celebrities of the day. I say surprising, as it was after all just a small town in the middle of the Algerian desert.

One day I was called to the gate where I found an elderly American lady called Gladys Hight, on a tour of North Africa, who said she would like to visit the barracks and the museums. I translated to the RSM who gave me the necessary permission and I showed her around. I then accepted her invitation to dinner at the Continental Hotel, the only reasonable hotel for Europeans in the town at that time. I suppose that she was in the late forties but she was good fun and enjoyed playing cards. I took a few days leave and we toured the countryside, all at her expense, by taxi and bus. She gave me a signed photograph that I carried with me as far as Indochina where it got lost, on the back of which it indicated that she owned the Gladys Hight School of Dancing in New York and one of her pupils, famous even then, was the star of *Singing in the Rain,* Gene Kelly.

One of the most important visitors of that period, for me, was Maurice Chevalier, the great French entertainer and Hollywood actor. He came to visit the Music of the Legion when he was performing for one night only at the Empire Cinema. The orchestra was rehearsing for the Sunday concert and I got into conversation with his manager and found that he came from just a few miles from where I had been born in County Durham. I was given the day off to escort Mr Chevalier and his manager around the Legion and the town. We had drinks and lunch together and I was then invited to attend his concert at the Empire. The very next day they all left for Morocco.

Another memorable visitor was the wonderful Josephine Baker, who was performing at the local cinema. I had the good fortune of spending an afternoon with her, showing her around the barracks and Sidi-bel-Abbès. We then had dinner together and I watched her show from the wings. At the end of her performance, she turned towards me and announced to the audience, who appeared to love her almost as much as I did by then, that the next song was for *le petit Anglais* who had been so kind to her during her unforgettable visit to the Legion. During the German occupation of France, Josephine Baker worked with the Red Cross and the French Resistance, and entertained troops in North Africa. After the war, she was awarded the Croix de Guerre and the Rosette de la Résistance and was named a Chevalier of the Légion d honneur by Charles de Gaulle.

On one occasion a detachment of the Navy returned a few days after their first visit with the complete uniform of a Petty Officer in the Navy in their taxi. They wanted me to put the uniform on and they would see to it that I got on board their ship in Oran and that would be it as far as my time in the Legion was concerned. I thanked them but refused to co-operate. It still strikes me as funny that so many people thought I was in the Legion under some kind of duress and saw it as their mission to 'save me'. On another occasion a taxi arrived with two young lads and two young girls from the West End of London. This was really going to be a lark. They had come in a private plane that had landed at Sidi-bel-Abbès flying field and had announced that they would like to visit the Legion as they had heard that a young Englishman was there to show them around. They too were taken with the notion of rescuing me and had concocted a dramatic escape where I would slip under the seats or into the boot of the taxi and away we would go to the airfield where there was neither security nor customs. There would be nothing to it! Next stop Spain and then back to good old Britain. Where they had got their information about me, I do not know, although I suppose it might not have been me they were after. I never found out. Needless to say, I stayed in the Legion.

6

Journeying to Join the War

Whon war was declared, as in other Regiments, the *Musique* was discontinued. Musical instruments were stored away and the musicians sent to the various companies as stretcher-bearers or hospital orderlies as is usual. But again, I was given a plum job as librarian in the *Foyer du Légionnaire* although I also had to serve as part-time batman to RSM Oscar Schmidt, an Alsatian, who was in charge of the running of the Foyer. He was a quiet, efficient NCO, who had some fifteen years' service in the Legion so had seen numerous campaigns in North Africa. He was not demanding at all and I was able to carry on with my English lessons.

Indeed, I was able to completely reorganise the library so that it became much more popular with the men. There was only one occasion that I can remember when I had any trouble. It was when Biscotti, an Italian, took umbrage at some remark that I had made about the Italians and he came at me with a knife. In front of quite a crowd in the bar of the Foyer, I took care of Biscotti and his knife with short shrift and he was carried off to his bed.

It was during this short period that several officers came to see me for English conversation lessons. Among them was Captain Amilakvari, a Georgian nobleman who was to die most bravely in the Western Desert in 1942 fighting for the Free French forces, and Captain Komaroff who was to die in my arms in Indochina in 1945. It was a most remarkable part of my life for I was among the very few men with a signed authorisation by the Colonel permitting us to go into town on a bicycle with a rifle across one's back and five rounds in a pouch, with bayonet sheathed at one's side.

But the desire to serve my country was strong and I wanted to leave this sheltered life and do something different. Not knowing what was going to happen as far as the Legion was concerned, I wrote to the American *Chargé d'Affaires* in Algiers who was dealing with British matters at the time, to see if there was any possibility of my getting back to Britain. He replied that he had received no instructions as far as Englishmen in the Legion were concerned so there was nothing he could do. But then an instruction was issued by the Colonel calling for volunteers for Narvik in Norway and I immediately put my name on the list. I was called into the Colonel's office to be told that I would not be going. The battalion going to Narvik would be going via Liverpool and the Legion would then lose me to the British Army which they did not want to do. I was disappointed as it seemed that there was nothing I could do to enter the struggle against Nazi Germany.

In June 1940 France fell and shortly afterwards I heard from my friend Tétaert in the Colonel's office that the Germans had established a Commission at Algiers. They were to investigate the Legion records to discover the Germans who had 'deserted' their Fatherland as well as all one-time nationals of those countries aligned against them. This would of course include myself and any other légionnaires serving as British, Dutch, Belgian etc. It also included any Jewish légionnaires; *'Engagés volontaires pour la durée de la guerre'* (volunteers joined up only for the duration of the war). We were in the hands of the Colonel and it was a precarious time. However, he acted against the orders of the Vichy Government who had decided to collaborate with the Nazi conquerors and we were safe, for the time being.

In April 1941, a final detachment for the Far East and Tonking was organised and this was to be my ticket out of the North African desert. The detachment was purportedly to relieve those légionnaires with the 5th Regiment who had come to the end of their engagements or who were too sick to continue with the Legion and had to be repatriated. It was certainly a melting pot of nationalities, men united in their wish to fight against the

Nazis. It was composed of those Germans who did not wish to fall into the hands of the Nazis because of political or moral opposition, one English-speaking Russian called Ross engaged as British, one English-speaking German called Stern engaged as Canadian, for he had worked in Canada for some time, several others of various nationalities who were anti-Nazi and many Jews, really fleeing for their lives. There was just the one true Englishman; myself. The detachment numbered two hundred and fifty men and two officers. The officers were Captain Tokhadze, the senior, who was a white Russian and in charge and Lieutenant Pepin-Lehalleur who used to be my instruction officer at Saïda. They both spoke a little English.

Together with seven hundred and fifty Indochinese who had been involved in the defence of France and were being returned to their homes, we left Sidi-bel-Abbès in late April 1941 and went by train towards Morocco, via Oujda on the Algerian/Moroccan frontier. It began as a very uncomfortable journey in poor conditions. The train travelled very slowly with frequent stops and we were not allowed off the train at any time. We were on iron rations and there was no buffet car.

Although it was against the rules, I eventually made my way along the corridor of the train and arrived at the first-class carriages where I recognised someone who probably did not wish to be recognised. Jean Pierre Aumont was at that time one of the most famous film stars in France and there he was with a famous female film star whose name I conveniently forget. Excusing myself I entered the compartment and asked for his autograph on a postcard addressed to my family in England that I had all ready to post in Casablanca, our embarking destination. Jean Pierre noticed the address and immediately suggested I sit down and talk with them. I asked if I could go and ask my Section Sergeant for permission, which I did, then I returned and spent the rest of the journey very pleasantly indeed for they were allowed to descend at stops to purchase food and drink.

According to an issue of the *Nice Matin* in 1994 which covered the fiftieth anniversary celebrations of D-Day, Jean Pierre Aumont had been called up after the declaration of war in 1939. When his division was pushed down through France to Bordeaux he was demobilised and made his way to the United States in 1942 where he continued acting and began working for MGM. He then decided to return to Europe to join the Free French but they asked him to stay in Hollywood and help fight the cause by starring in a film about the Free French who were joining General de Gaulle. The film was called *The Cross of Lorraine* and it was completed in 1943. The same year he married a well-known actress, Maria Montez, and was immediately sent to fight in North Africa as a cadet-officer. He served as Aide-de-Camp to General Brosset and moved with the Allied Armies through Italy and France. His bravery earned him the Légion d'Honneur and the Croix de Guerre. In his memoirs, *Le Soleil at les Ombres* (The Sun and the Shadows) he tells of the time at Naples on the 8th August 1940 when he saw Churchill, in a very small boat, saluting the troops with the V sign '....it looked as if he was giving us his benediction'. The *Nice Matin* devoted a whole page to Pierre Aumont but there was nothing to explain how on earth he happened to be on a train going to Casablanca in 1941. I wonder too if he remembers *le petit Anglais*.

In Casablanca we were in appalling conditions, stuffed into a shed near the docks waiting for the *Dupleix* to be ready for us. I was able to visit an ex-Légionnaire friend who was a master printer with the local newspaper. We had dinner together with his wife before I returned to the docks. It was three o'clock in the morning. No sooner did I collect my things and resume my Legion identity (I had removed my uniform jacket, puttees and equipment before going out) than we were ready to go. We marched to a narrow wooden gangway with ropes stretched on either side, reaching from the quayside up to a hole in the side of the 7,000-ton coal-burning cargo ship at an angle approaching sixty degrees. It was early morning. I began to climb. In front of me was an elderly, pro-British, Belgian friend, named Merx. He was very drunk, which was his usual condition when off duty. I closed up on him in view of his state, and it was just as well that I did, for when he was just more than half-way up, he slipped through the ropes up the side of the gangway, falling towards the dark, very dirty, oil-covered waters below. As he passed me I made a grab for his equipment and managed to find a firm hold. I held on for grim death till our companions behind me lent their hands and we got him back safely onto the ladder and safety. Then the Indochinese were embarked and shown to their quarters, a deck below ourselves; we were two decks below the main deck. Tiers of bunks had been rapidly constructed to house us. There was not much room to move and it was most uncomfortable, even alongside. What it was going to be like during the next hundred days I just refused to contemplate. We were getting away from Nazi commission, and that was the main point.

Once on board I was put in charge of creating a library. Before leaving Sidi-bel-Abbès I had been told to pack a few hundred books for the voyage and so, with my camp-bed near the library, a wooden box-like construction amidships on the second deck, I was pretty comfortable. I was also in charge of the board games and so, when my friends wanted to play chess, or cards, there were no problems, we played. I organised bridge, chess and *belote* tournaments and so life in general was not really too boring. However, the food was a different story. After the first few days of fresh-ish beef and pork, the meals became rather repetitive with salt fish and rice being the main ingredients for all meals. Whilst this was not ideal for the légionnaires, the Indochinese, who had their own kitchen staff, seemed very happy with the continuous fish and rice diet for it was what they were used to. The problem for them arose when the weather got bad, which was pretty often in the South Atlantic and the Indian Ocean. Their eating and sleeping quarters were forward and the kitchen aft of the bridge which they had to cross to get their food. Their only road between the two was up a steel stairway, along the bridge, and down another stairway on the other side. Most of the time, before achieving the stairways, they just squirmed along the deck pushing the hot containers before them. We did sympathise with them but we could do nothing about it. They too were very crowded as they had been allotted only a small portion of the deck where they could get any fresh air. They spent their days playing a type of *mahjong* or listening to stories read to them from a book written in Indochinese. These were apparently tales of brave deeds performed by legendary heroes. Many of them spent hours with tweezers plucking the hairs from their chins and faces as they never shaved. Several officers accompanied them to organise patrols during the voyage to stop homosexual practices which were rife and there were quite a number of légionnaires willing to pay to participate. It always amazed me to see how beautiful some of the Indochinese men were, especially the *métisses,* i.e. those of mixed blood.

As mentioned before, Churchill did not trust the Germans, or Admiral Darlan, Commander of the French Navy, and felt it was vital to make sure that the two modern French battleships, *Richelieu* and *Jean Bart* should not fall into the hands of the Germans for, with the *Bismarck* about to be commissioned in August, the trio would present a formidable line of battle against the Allies. The Franco-German armistice was signed on 24th June and the Atlantic ports of France were to be occupied by the Germans but not the Mediterranean ones. The *Richelieu* lay at Dakar and as the French Admiral had refused conditions proposed to him by the British, in July 1940, a launch manned by British personnel entered the port and seriously damaged the battleship by exploding depth charges against her hull. Naval aircraft also attacked the boat and the damage caused by the two methods immobilised the *Richelieu* for two and a half years. Our first stop was in

Dakar where we were to take on as much fresh food as possible and the first thing we saw was the *Richelieu* with a great big hole just above the waterline in the bows.

On board *Dupleix,* in case of emergencies, there were two huge fresh-water containers positioned on deck. We had been lucky in our journey as far as Dakar and had not run into any kind of trouble, but then a real disaster struck, and it had nothing to do with the enemy. We had left the coast of Africa and sailed south avoiding the known shipping lanes which were being scoured by three German battleships, the *Gneisenau, Scharnhorst* and *Hipper,* when the Captain found that the ship was listing badly to port. He immediately called the chief engineer who found that he had his work cut out coaxing the ancient engines to do their work. He gave the job to the third engineer (the second was resting after his night watch duties) who was engaged in some important work trying to get the electric lights working before nightfall. He gave the job to the fourth engineer who had become my friend as he spoke quite good English. The job was to transfer some of the seawater we were carrying as ballast from the port to the starboard side in order to correct the list. It was felt that the list was due to the fact that the ship was without a cargo as the agents had not been able to find anything suitable for this dangerous trip. Unfortunately, my friend was not a marine man at all; he had just left university and wished to join his parents in Shanghai where his father was the Manager of the Franco-Chinese bank. Haiphong was more or less on the way. So, my naive friend pushed the wrong button with the result that, although the list was corrected, the salt water got mixed up with the fresh water on board. We were obliged to rely on the two tanks on deck. No more fresh water for showers or ablutions for anybody and an armed guard had to be placed on the now locked tanks with every drop of fresh water being severely rationed till we reached Madagascar.

Shipping in the region of the Cape of Good Hope was very congested because, I reasoned, there was so much activity from the belligerents in the Mediterranean and vessels therefore preferred the much longer route via the Cape. As a result, we on board the *Dupleix,* were obliged to steam some four hundred additional miles, so I was told by my friend the 4th engineer, south of the Cape into very cold Antarctic waters. Here it was decidedly unpleasant and the Indochinese men particularly suffered as they were not used to such cold weather and rough seas. It was a relief for all of us when we turned north-east towards Tamatave (now Toamasina) in Madagascar where everything was lovely with warm sunshine, balmy breezes and wooded hills.

Seasickness was another tribulation we had to endure. One of the NCOs had been terribly seasick on a previous cruise to the Far East that went through the Suez Canal, but as Tonkin was considered to be the Eden of Legion life, he was quite prepared to suffer again. This was going to be a much longer voyage even though the bush telegraph had informed us that the Allies were going to allow free passage to the *Dupleix* as far as Saïgon, for we were not carrying any war material. Therefore, with the co-operation of one of the crew, the NCO worked out the exact centre of gravity of the ship and lay down on a mattress as near as possible to this spot, prepared to spend as much time as possible there. I never found out if it worked or not.

Madagascar lies two hundred and forty miles off the east coast of Africa, opposite Mozambique, and is the fourth largest island in the world. Its area of 227,760 square miles is almost completely within the boundaries of the tropics. It is surrounded by small volcanic islands, the Comoro and Mascarene Islands and the Seychelles.

The island was certainly inhabited by Indonesians and Indians (from the Indian sub-continent) during the Iron Age but for many years the island was inhabited by a variety of peoples separated by uninhabited stretches of country and included many who came from across the Mozambique Straits; they were Arabs or Moslems of various origins. Various European powers tried to convert the inhabitants and to take possession of the island including the Portuguese, the British and the French who, under Charles I, claimed sovereignty. In 1890, in return for certain interests on the mainland of Africa, Britain recognised it as a French Protectorate. Nevertheless, this did not stop British connivance with the Malagasy Prime Minister against the French and there was trouble. In 1895, an expeditionary force, with at least two battalions of the Foreign Legion, was sent to Majunga, on the north-west coast, to march to Tananarive (Antananarivo) to establish the Protectorate more firmly. In 1896, there was a rebellion, not only anti-French but also anti-Christian and General Gallieni, the Governor-General abolished Royalty on the island. Gallieni proved himself a very just and understanding Governor as far as the islanders were concerned and he was well liked. Lots of islanders who were loyal and serving in the administration were made French citizens. He retired in 1905. In 1940, the island declared for the Vichy Government and to prevent it being taken over by the Japanese it was occupied by the British in 1942 before being handed over to the Free French in 1943. My visit was in 1941, and we were told of many memorials on the island erected to honour the Legion Officers and men who had died on duty there. However, when our detachment arrived in Tamatave, no permits were to be issued because a previous Legion detachment had been allowed to land and had created havoc when the légionnaires got very drunk.

On the first morning there, I suddenly developed a very violent attack of toothache, necessitating, with Captain Tokhadze's blessing, a visit to the dentist at the hospital. The visit lasted all day, and still the dentist could not discover the cause of my trouble. I was sent on my way with a small bottle of Sloan's liniment to rub on my gums. This was actually a ruse and allowed me the opportunity to have a look around the town which I found most interesting. I had to keep off the main streets as much as possible and out of the way of the police but I did spend some time in the Catholic church and made the acquaintance of a lovely, accommodating young Malgache girl who lunched with me at a French restaurant where they accepted my French francs. I managed to obtain a bottle of whisky to present to Captain Tokhadze on my return, much to his surprise. I also purchased a few second-hand novels for the library, which went down very well with my superiors and my fellow travellers. After revictualling and taking on fresh water which was most essential, we then sailed north again to the end of the island and tied up in Diego Suarez harbour (now Antsiranana), where coal was available. The air was filled with coal dust all day.

I noticed that there was a medium-sized cargo ship in the port, flying the American flag. I hailed a rowing boat and sent a message across by the boatman asking if they had any reading material to spare for a lonely Englishman. The boat returned laden with paperbacks and an invitation for me to take a couple of friends to the ship for dinner. I took some of the books to Captain Tokhadze and asked for permission to accept the invitation and to take two English-speaking men with me. Trusting me, he gave me permission and together with a German who had lived in Canada for some time and an English-speaking Russian, we smartened ourselves up as much as possible and were rowed across the waters.

On board we had a fine time and two master cooks who also happened to be twins, gave us a splendid dinner. All the American officers were ashore and in fact, there were only the cooks on board. They did not know how long they were going to be in the port. I tried to persuade them to hide us and take us off to join the British forces somewhere but they were adamant that there was nothing they could do. I suppose we didn't really expect them to help us for we all knew that if we had stayed aboard there we would have been posted as deserters and the Malgache police would have been after us as soon as they were informed. We rejoined the *Dupleix* at about 10pm taking with us a load of *Cokes* which were much appreciated. At that time, US ships were dry, although I do remember going on board the American aircraft-carrier *Randolph* in the Mediterranean with Sir Winston Churchill in the 1950s and permission had been obtained from the White House (President Eisenhower) for several cases of champagne to be brought aboard from Cannes, so that Sir Winston and his party could enjoy their visit.

At midnight we heard the siren of the American ship sounding loud and long and there appeared to be a lot of commotion on its deck. I caught a glimpse of someone waving as she disappeared out of the port.

Whilst on board the American ship I had asked to see maps of the supposed route of the *Dupleix* and had noticed that the closest we would be to land was when we went through the Sunda Strait between Java and Sumatra. There were a number of islands in the vicinity, still under Dutch protection I hoped, and the Dutch were surely our allies. I might be able to do something there.

One of the lifeboats at the stern was loaded, I knew, with supplies necessary for several days afloat should the ship be sunk. I had made it my business to find this out and always kept thinking on how I might leave the Legion to find a way to join the British forces. Only five other légionnaires were in on my plan. I had identified the lifeboat as my possible escape route and I informed them only hours before I intended to do the jump. They included Corporal Frey, an Austrian with whom I had played many games of chess and bridge on the boat, the German-Canadian, a fair-haired Scandinavian, the Russian-born man and one other.

Another of our bridge and chess companions at the time was Borchers, a very intelligent character who was most reticent about his past. He was perfectly within his rights to be so and it turned out later that he had been a teacher in Germany and a fulltime member of the Communist party. He joined Frey in his later association with the Viet communists and when he returned to East Germany he became Head of the Radio Services there. But he was not one of the few I had chosen for my escape plans who all spoke reasonable English and who all seemed to be favourably disposed towards the British.

During the afternoon of the night that I had chosen for the escape, Captain Tokhadze issued orders for all the lifeboats to be guarded by armed Indochinese soldiers. Someone had spilled the beans. The next day, Tokhadze called me in to his cabin and reminded me that I had signed a contract for five years and as the Legion had kept its side of the bargain, I should do likewise. I suppose our good relationship meant that he did not feel the need to threaten me with punishment. But still I kept to my intentions.

The followed day we were through the Strait and entered Dutch waters. I waited for nightfall by an open porthole and with a torch I kept flashing an 'SOS I AM BRITISH' signal into the dark. The very next morning at about 10 o'clock, a Dutch patrol boat suddenly appeared from behind one of the small islands and signalled the *Dupleix* to heave-to. The ship stopped and a dinghy came over with two Dutch officers and three sailors, all heavily armed.

They climbed aboard to be met by the ship's captain and Captain Tokhadze. The Dutchmen did not speak French and our officers only spoke a little English so naturally I became escort to the Dutchmen and as we toured below I implored them to take me with them, adding that it really was their duty. They said that as they had no instructions as to what they should do with Englishmen in the French forces, they could not take me. I asked them what they would do if suddenly three or four of us jumped into the sea. They said that if the sharks did not get us, they would fish us out and return us to the *Dupleix*. They returned to their ship and sailed off. Another attempt had failed.

When we arrived in Saigon, after one hundred and seven days of sailing from Casablanca, we were confined to barracks ashore while the ship was cleaned up and restocked for the next part of the voyage. I bribed the Colonial Sergeant of the guard to let me out for a few hours and went to see the acting British Consul-General, Mr. Meiklereid. He told me, as had the others, that he could do nothing about getting me to British forces. However, he had a very good reason. The whole city, particularly the docks area, was patrolled by the Japanese who were there by permission of the Vichy Government. We were in enemy territory. There was no way out.

I had dinner at the Consulate, we had a few hands of bridge with friends of the Consul who happened to turn up, more talk and then I returned to the barracks, having to sneak back in over the wall. Looking back, I suppose it was rather a strange evening – playing cards in the Consulate building, in an occupied territory and then having to sneak back to base. Mr Meiklereid kindly sent a letter to my parents via the Diplomatic bag to let them know that I was in fine fettle. I still have the letter.

A couple of days later we were on our way up through the South-China Seas towards Haiphong. The approach to the port was a most beautiful scene, with dozens of small islands in the Bay of Along, all covered with the most remarkably shaped trees.

On arrival in the port of Haiphong I soon discovered that there were another 50,000 Japanese in the Tanking area (North Vietnam) but we had no trouble as we took the train for Hanoi and Vietri, the headquarters of the 5th Regiment of the Legion. In Vietri I was given yet another clerical job; in the office dealing with all the material issued to the whole Regiment. My direct boss for a few months was ex-Adjutant Henninger, and for a while life continued to be rather quiet. I suppose I should have been grateful for the horrors of war would soon be upon me and my new colleagues. Henninger would be taken prisoner by the Japanese in 1945 and would be subjected to unspeakable torture and malnutrition. The action I had so longed for was looming and would change me forever.

7
Indochina

When I arrived in Indochina (Vietnam) in 1941, it consisted of the French protectorates of Tonking, Annam, Cambodia and Laos and the French colony of Cochin-China. It was bound on the north by the Chinese provinces of Yunnan and Kwangsi, to the south and east by the South China Sea, and to the West by Siam (Thailand) and the eastern part of Burma. Today this area is known as Vietnam, Cambodia and Laos. The people in the eastern area were Annamites; in Cambodia they were Khmer; in Laos were the Thai. There were also many different groups of aboriginal peoples speaking Malayo-Polynesian languages like the Cham, the Moi and the Kha whom the dominating peoples at that time referred to as 'savages'. It seems that the prejudices of colonialism have long roots.

The undeclared war between the Japanese and the Chinese had begun in 1931 and by 1939 the Japanese were well established in Chinese territories and occupied all the major seaports so that China could only get its supplies by overland routes. In 1939, this changed again and supplies were delivered from the Indochinese port of Haiphong either via the railways or the Burma Road. After France fell in 1940, the Japanese demanded the closure of the Burma Road to which Churchill agreed to a three months temporary closure. At a similar time, the French Vichy Government agreed to the Japanese use of bases in Tonkin – purportedly for their operations against the Chinese. In reality this meant the termination of any supplies getting through to China via Haiphong or the railway through the mountains. The Japanese stranglehold increased and by 1941 it not only had control of Indochina's transport system but on two of its biggest exports; rice and rubber. Meanwhile Siam had attacked the weaker Laos and Cambodia and through Vichy-inspired Japanese intervention certain Laotian provinces lying to the west of the Mekong and a large part of western Cambodia had been ceded to the Siamese in March 1941.

Churchill did nothing. Some may argue that he did worse than nothing as he stopped several French attempts to send reinforcements to its colony. He was already in deep trouble with the Vichy Government because of the attacks on the French Fleet at Dakar and Mers-el-Kébir which had also raised opposition from his naval colleagues at home even if it had strengthened the British public's confidence in his determination to win the war. He declined to send much needed aircraft to the defence of Singapore and other British possessions in the Far East. The main objective, as far as Churchill was concerned, was Hitler. I wonder what would have happened had Churchill sent some of the thousands of tanks that he despatched to Russia and the Western Desert, to Malaya? Would Singapore have fallen? I think so, for Singapore was the flower of the British Empire out there and its capture would always have been a great triumph for the Rising Sun, however many men it took to take it.

On Bastille Day, 14 July 1941, the Japanese demanded and were ceded by Vichy, eight airfields and two ports, including Saigon. According to their message to Vichy, they were in occupation to prevent an occupation by De Gaulle and the British. When the United States, Holland and Britain froze their assets and put an embargo on the export of oil and raw materials, Japan mobilised all its forces. Arriving in Vietri in Indochina in 1941 as a British member of the French Foreign Legion was therefore rather complicated.

Despite war and international power play raging all around, on my arrival in Vietri, the HQ of the 5th Regiment of the Foreign Legion, I was yet again given a clerical job. This was in the *Bureau du Matériel* (Ordnance Office) where I had to keep up to date records detailing each and every piece of armament, ammunition, equipment, as well as animals and boots – in fact everything except food, but including all kitchen equipment. This was for the entire Regiment which had sections and companies scattered all over Tonking. As usual, it was a job I was pushed into without there being any question of asking me whether I liked it or not, so I made sure, also as usual, that I was going to do a good job, and if possible, to enjoy it. I was able, however, to request to be allowed to participate in guard duties, parades and even manoeuvres for I was still a légionnaire. From the very start I understood why old soldiers had spoken about Indochina being the Paradise of the Legion; in the dining rooms and in the offices, *boys* (room servants), *be cons* (assistants) or *beps* (kitchen lads) did all the work and it was most pleasant. Although, as a first-class soldier with one green stripe on each arm, I still had to do the things that I had been used to in North Africa.

The majority of légionnaires always hope they will have no commitments at Christmas time. There are no parades, except for Guard and no visits by Generals or Ministers. There is extra food and wine, and entertainment; so rare in those days in the life of a légionnaire. When the food and wine are good, the sick parade is short and there is less *cafard* for the men are happier. *Le cafard* is actually a cockroach, but in colloquial terms in the Legion, it means that you are quite browned off. The Legion's cure for the *cafard* is manoeuvres, marches, drill, guard duty, danger, or entertainment. As a result, wherever you find the Legion at Christmas you will find the old-fashioned music hall.

As Christmas drew near in that year of 1941, volunteers were called to take part in the traditional show. When volunteers are called for in the Legion everyone steps forward. You can imagine what happens to those who do not: extra guard duties, confined to barracks, sweeping the square and the quarters or even sweeping the six floors of stairs with several toothbrushes as I did on one occasion in Sidi-bel-Abbès when I failed to volunteer for some job I thought I would dislike.

Then the NCOs in charge (as it really is the NCOs that run the Legion while the officers, though thoroughly efficient in all ways, keep an eye on things from a distance) got together a small committee to decide what form the entertainment was to take. Weeding out then followed and most of the volunteers went back to their companies while, on this occasion Hungarians, Austrians, Germans, Italians, French, and one Englishman, yours truly, remained. The show was to be held as usual in the Foyer, the hall containing what our own forces would call the NAAFI, seating about two hundred people under a tin roof, on hard metal chairs, just outside the barrack gates so that visitors did not have to go through the procedure of passing the Guardhouse into the barracks. Behind the Foyer at Vietri was a large lake full of carp which was dredged every six months or so with the resultant muddy catch being passed to the Commissariat to supplement normal rations.

Three or four days before Christmas everything was organised and the first performance could begin. We did the show on three nights; the first being for the ordinary soldiers stationed in the area, not only the Legion but from the Colonial Regiment, the Artillery and the Air Force from Kim Dai, some five or six miles away. The second night was for the NCOs and their guests and the final night for VIPs, Officers and their guests.

The show of that year began with rifle drill on stage. A dozen of us were dressed as tin soldiers. In the Legion we had men who had pursued almost every profession or vocation under the sun and included a number of skilled tailors so all our costumes were made to measure and we were a very smart troop of tin soldiers marching up and down and across the stage to the tune of 'The March of the Tin Soldiers'. The audience joined in with whistles and loud voices which almost drowned out the sound of the orchestra of the 5th

Regiment which was seated in front of the raised stage and separated from the audience by a dark, chest-high curtain. It was all very professional, as was everything the Legion did, and still does. Our leader for this particular group was Peps Pyl from the Austrian Tyrol, one of the smartest men I ever knew, who was the Sergeant in charge of PT at that time. Our friendship lasted many years and I came to know him by three different names; the first in the Legion, later with a second name when we worked in the Resistance and finally, when we met again in Paris after the war, it came as no surprise that he had married a Baroness and thus had inherited a title. After the drill came a selection of Schubert songs from another Austrian, Lance-Sergeant Bruckner, a man I disliked intensely and who was so very different from his fellow-national, my friend Pyl. But Bruckner always gave a superb rendering of Schubert's dreamy songs and my dislike of him was forgotten for that day. He even looked a bit like Schubert, but was very pro-Nazi, which didn't help our relationship much.

For my next appearance I was billed as *Yarrum – Prestidigitateur* (Yarrum being Murray reversed), and I performed magic and mindreading. My partner in my mindreading act was Hubner, a German who spoke excellent French having spent a number of years in Paris. I do not know how he got into the Legion – a bastion of masculinity as, for this act, he was dressed as a Parisian *cocotte*, and even walked like one, with alarming proficiency! With silk stockings, corset, high-heeled shoes, black lace dress, a terrific Parisian hat (made by one of the afore-mentioned tailors) and remarkable make-up; Hubner was the most attractive European we had seen for many months. Blindfolded with a thick black bandeau that had been passed round for examination before the act, 'Madame Yvette' sat, very much admired by the audience on a high stool with just the right amount of thigh showing. I touched various members of the audience on their heads, one at a time, with my magic wand calling out in a sepulchral voice "Who is *this* person"...

in French of course. My first selection of a muleteer drew the husky reply from Madame that she could smell animals and began to sing a rather spicy song about the Cavalry of the Legion: *"Ma bonne étoile a voulu, que je viens à la Montée .faire le cavalier..."* (My lucky star decided that I should join the Cavalry...to be a cavalier) and there was much understanding applause. I made several other choices and similarly witty responses issued from the lovely lips of my medium.

Our audience was enthralled and as I expected, just when I was about to conclude, CSM Driesch, a well-known disciplinarian, stood up and implored me to touch his head with my wand. Driesch and I got on very well together. He had a great facility for foreign languages and in addition to his native German, he could speak with a great degree of fluency, English, French, Hungarian, Spanish and Arabic. He had once been a trainee priest and had been educated at Heidelberg University. I do not know why he joined the Legion for that was a question never asked. I did as he asked and he was very surprised indeed at the amount of personal information that my medium brought forth, much to the amusement of the audience.

The next act was a group of Hungarian dancers, resplendent in their beautiful white blouses, red velvet boleros, voluminous white trousers tied tight at the ankles, white socks and pointed slippers. These men were not very tall, but giants in valour when the fight with the Japanese came. At the Christmas show they danced like the true Tziganes they were; up and down, round and round, leaping, swirling, sweating. All the while the fiddles played and the accordion raced along in rhythm. The home-made pipes of Pan bubbled with the joy of it all as the tambourines rattled to the *czardas* and the dancers followed the music from slow to fast and faster and faster to a final sudden, stamping stop. The General himself led the audience in a tumultuous standing ovation.

After the first interval the Russian choir gave a grand performance of

Volga laments and folk-songs to break the hearts of even the most hardened soldiers, while Lieutenant Elyseev, forty-five years old at least, and Private Popov, probably a bit older, gave a superb exhibition of Cossack dances. Before joining the Legion, Elyseev had been the Colonel in command of the famous White Russian Cossack Riding School in the Ukraine until the Bolsheviks forced him to flee his country. The Russians in the Legion were a fine crowd; friends with everybody, terrific drinkers, grand soldiers whether drunk or sober and always ready for an adventure. The Russian choir, and on occasions I was conscripted for they were short of tenors, was always a great success and annually toured northern Indochina for charity. After the choir came a short two-act play *Le Commissaire est Bon Enfant* (The Chief of Police is not a Bad Guy) with my friend Driesch playing the Chief of Police who was quite mad. Then came the second break. These breaks were very important for the weather was hot and sticky and singing, talking and laughing was warm work.

At last came *Murray and His Boys* as we were billed on the programme. I had with me Bertolotti, an Italian who sang well and played the accordion; Hubner who had assisted me during my magic act who had a good singing voice – and no, not contralto - and Schroeder who played the guitar. Schroeder had studied at La Sorbonne in Paris where he soon became a Reader, but he saw the war coming, the unpreparedness of France and the approaching pogrom, so he joined the Legion for the duration of the war and was sent to Indochina. He was not a good soldier but a very good secretary in the Major's office. We were all very surprised when he turned out to be one of our very best cross-country runners. We often played chess together and bridge with other colleagues. He was also a gifted pianist. The Legion really was the biggest melting pot of talent from around the world.

Anyone in the Legion who spoke English was, it was commonly believed, related to the cowboys of the USA. So, we dressed accordingly and as such were a great success with *Goodbye Hawaii, Rosie the Redskin, South of the Border* and *Auld Lang Syne* (*Le Chant d'Adieu*). That Christmas Eve, as always with the Legion, the whole audience joined us to finish with *Le Boudin*, the Legion's anthem. Quite a lot of my colleagues tried to cram forty-eight hours or more of celebrating into that one day of Christmas, forgetting for a while that war was raging. Boxing Day, which was not a holiday, was to follow the next day as surely as the sun was going to rise and was to give no rest to those well-earned headaches.

With Christmas over, Legion life returned to normal. As soon as I was able to, I volunteered for the very difficult and exhausting school for Corporals and then again as soon as I was promoted I obtained permission to go in for the Sergeant's Training Course at Tong. This involved gruelling day and night marches, orienteering, shooting, climbing mountains, obstruction courses and reconnaissance work. I found that I developed some skill in making and reading maps and sketches of the terrain which would prove to be very useful in future warfare.

Early in 1943, before appearing in orders which would announce that I had passed my exams, I was called into Colonel Alessandri's office to be told that I had been chosen to be *Professeur d'Anglais* at the newly-established Military Academy at Tong. Tong is some 40km from Hanoi, and the EMIA (*Ecole Militaire d'Infanterie et d'Artillerie*) had resuscitated the crack military academies of St Cyr, St Maixent and Poitiers, which had been completely destroyed by the Nazis when Paris fell in 1940. It had been decided, by the powers that be, that there was great need for a military academy to be formed in order to provide officers for the army. Due to the important effectives of the Legion, the Colonial Infantry, the Colonial Artillery and the various native regiments in Indochina, coupled with the impossibility of replacements being sent from France, this seemed like a useful and worthwhile enterprise. The Legion provided several of the instructors, myself included. I was immediately promoted to Lance-Sergeant and became a full Sergeant within weeks. This meant that now I had a *boy* to do all the chores in a room where I had the company of only two other Sergeants. I had my meals in the Sergeants' Mess where the food was even better than in the soldiers' refectory, even though I had to pay for it from my much-increased monthly salary.

Within a very short time, I augmented this salary even more by giving private English lessons to young Chinese and Indochinese lads studying for their diplomas. During these lessons I learned quite a lot of Chinese expressions that were to come in very useful later when we entered Chinese territory during the Great Retreat. I only had two or three young ladies as pupils, two of them the daughters of our Colonel Alessandri, and the other was a *métisse* – half European, half Indochinese, called Giovanangeli. Her father was a senior warden at the Hanoi prison. Years later she was to see an article in a French newspaper about me being Churchill's bodyguard and she wrote to me care of the Hotel de Paris in Monte Carlo. She had married and was then living in Marseilles, close to her parents. They had all apparently been taken as prisoners of war by the Japanese and had suffered considerably.

In Tong, Giovanangeli's family had lived in the same square as me. By this time, I had taken on a *congaï* or *cô*, (concubine) who looked after nearly all my needs, especially the extra food I required, for I was young and very energetic. What can I say about Nguyen Thi Sec, this intelligent young girl who was originally from Cochin-China in the far south of the country? The third daughter of the Nguyen family, she was beautiful, very dainty and conducted herself at all times in the nicest possible way. Like most Indochinese she was very devout with regards to her family and ancestors and therefore she was happy that I did not mind her going to the local shrines to pray for them. On feast days she would go to pay the local priest to say prayers. Every month, when she received the money I gave her (I was apparently generous compared with other *Dôi tây* (European Sergeants)) she paid the local scribe to write a letter to her father in Soctrang, Cochin China, enclosing most of the money for the family. She could read Indochinese and kept me well-informed on native matters, but could not write although she was learning to. Cô Thi was a superb young lady and, as far as I could see and discover, was quite faithful to me, whereas most of the other *côs* were known to extend their favours more freely.

When I was on guard duty I could always rely on Cô Thi to bring along half a chicken or pork chops, for instance, with chips and cake and a flask of coffee (I used to get the real stuff from a Chinese merchant whose son was one of my pupils) at a pre-arranged time. She kept our *câi-nha* (two-roomed terraced cabin) and herself, scrupulously clean and always kept me informed on everything that went on in the village and the town of Tong. Above all, I think she felt she was lucky for I did not beat her or misuse her in any way as was the wont of most of the soldiers who had *côs*. She was well paid for her co-operation. Thi Sec also taught me quite a lot of her own language, but best of all we used to go gathering herbs, leaves and grasses out in the nearby countryside to be used in her excellent cuisine. This knowledge came in so handy when we were retreating towards China in 1945. Neither I myself, nor any member of my section went down with *béri-béri* thanks to Cô Thi. I often think of her with appreciation and hope and pray that her life after I had disappeared was not too difficult and that the Japanese were not too cruel to those civilians who remained in Tong after we had gone. I feel obliged to mention here that my relationship with Thi Sec was, as far as I was concerned, entirely a matter of mutual benefit, without any deep sentiment. I paid her for her services and she kept me well-fed, with the variety that I myself asked for and got, and which was not available in the Mess. With her there was also very little, or none at all, risk of venereal diseases so prevalent among soldiers in the Far East.

Another friend I had at that time was Maréchal de Logis Chef Debas (CSM in the *Remonte,* the French Army Service that deals with the training and replacement of officers' horses). He came from Clermont Ferrand in the Auvergne region of France and taught equestrianism to the officers from the Academy, so we had many mutual friends. Occasionally horses broke legs and had to be shot and it was Debas who had to do it, for he was also the veterinary surgeon. He would then telephone me in the Company office or leave a note somewhere asking me to visit him in his own office, just across the road from the Battalion Guard Room. These messages would arrive a couple of days after the death of the horse, so that Cô Thi and I, with friends perhaps if I was feeling generous, or the donor himself on occasions, could enjoy magnificent steaks from the huge piece of the haunch of the animal that Debas provided. Other edible parts of the animal would be passed over to the kitchen of the Colonial Regiment for he was after all, in the French Army. I developed a predilection for horse meat at the time and it has continued ever since although these days, since we left the London area, I find it quite impossible to find any.

Debas also taught me how to ride horses and again this proved a useful skill many years later when I accompanied Churchill on a trip to Morocco. From Marrakech we had flown some three hundred miles to Tinerhir, to paint the *Gorge du Todhra.* It is a superb place for any artist. We were met by a French Major in charge of native affairs. As we discussed security arrangements, he asked how it was that I spoke such good French and so my time in the Legion came into the conversation. The subject of Indochina also came up and my time at the Military Academy. This was of great interest to him for he and Major Carbonel, who was in command of the Academy, had spent time at St Cyr together and were of the same promotion of 1925. The Major told me that if I wanted anything, anything at all, I only had to ask. I asked for a couple of horses each morning so that Norman McGowan, Churchill's valet at the time, and myself could go riding out into the wild desert surrounding the *gîte d'étape*, the small hotel where we were staying. At 5.30am the very next morning, a couple of Mouquesni (native troops) appeared on horseback and brought with them two beautiful purebred Arab horses for Norman and myself. The Old Man was awake and immediately gave us permission to depart for an hour or so. It was fabulous and each morning Sir Winston would be at his window, overlooking the rough path leading up to the hotel to see us safely home.

On 7th December 1941, the Japanese attacked Pearl Harbor and declared war on the USA. The British and American declarations followed immediately. Somehow, I used to receive a Japanese-sponsored newsletter in English which gave news of the victories of the Japanese and other members of the AXIS alliance. However, from listening in to our own clandestine radio at the Academy, I knew these were totally untrue. The German campaign in Russia I remember was a complete farce yet, according to the Japanese newsletter, the defeat at Stalingrad became a superb German victory. Life in the Legion did not change perceptibly for the rank and file although at times it became very exciting for the few of us engaged on secretive sorties.

Around this time, I had a couple of days leave and decided to venture with a friend into the mountains to the east of Vietri, part of the Province of Vinh Yen. My friend was a German Jew called Fischer who had joined up, like so many others faced with persecution by Hitler's minions, for the duration of the war and with whom I had many unremitting games of chess. He was a good listener and didn't talk too much, in fact he was a most pleasant companion to travel with. We took with us bread, cold meat and a *bidon* of wine each, but we differed very much in our choice of wearing apparel. Whereas he wore a long-sleeved army shirt, buttoned to the neck, khaki linen knee-breeches, army issue, laced tightly below the knees, *bandes molletières* (puttees) and heavy regulation army boots, I wore a short-sleeved khaki shirt, shorts and sandals. We both wore *topees* (lightweight pith helmets) to protect us from the blazing summer sun that we would encounter in open spaces.

After a couple of hours or so we arrived at a small village set in a large clearing in the dense jungle, halfway up the mountain side. Here we were invited by the head of the village into his large *câi-nha* and served *chè* (tea) and *choum* (abbreviation of *ruou nêp choum* – rice alcohol).

The house was a very long, bamboo construction on wooden pillars, raised five or six feet above the ground and it housed all the members of his family numbering I estimated at between twenty and thirty people. The village was more or less self-supporting and appeared to be completely ignorant of the war in Europe. This I gleaned from the rather constrained conversation due to my lack of knowledge of their particular dialect, but I did understand that they had been visited by other foreigners, most certainly Japanese, some weeks previously. One or two of them did speak a bit of French which helped immensely, once they overcame their shyness, as years previously, they had worked in French military outposts in the area. I had picked up quite a lot of Annamese phrases from my *cô* and some Chinese expressions from my pupils, but they served practically no purpose at all for the Méos, like the other tribes in Indochina, the Moi, the Man, the Cham and the Muong to name but a few, have their own dialects and language which have no similarity to Annamese or Cochin-Chinese. However, sign language can, and indeed did, surmount most barriers.

Cattle, pigs and chickens were herded in stalls beneath the building and the farmyard atmosphere in the heat of the jungle was quite overpowering to us two Europeans. After sharing their communal meal of suckling pig, bean sprouts, bamboo shoots and green leaves very similar to our own spinach, we were escorted to another village about a mile away where we had another meal just as the sun was setting through the trees. We stayed in that village overnight, while young girls sang strange songs for hours and we drank much *choum* and *chè* and laughed and smiled to everything that was said to us. The atmosphere was most friendly and they seemed happy to receive the bundle of French *piastres* we gave them to repay them for the hospitality. How and when they were going to be able to spend it was their affair.

Quite early in the morning, with many *tchau dan ongs* and *tchau linh tais* (goodbye mister and goodbye French soldier) we hurried off for we had a long way to go back to Vietri. I led through the dense jungle where the humidity left me breathless and sweating even in my light garments. Fischer must have been experiencing an early trip to Purgatory. Just as I was about to place my hand on a tree-trunk that obstructed our path in order to leap over it, I suddenly saw, just in front of my outstretched hand, a vivid, beautiful, almost fluorescent green patch on the trunk. I hesitated. In sudden realisation of what it was I gasped and jumped back almost upsetting my companion who was close on my heels. What I had seen might be very beautiful, but it was also one of the most poisonous snakes in the Far East, the dreaded banana snake. How glad I was that I was not colour-blind. We eventually got back to barracks; tired, sweaty and hungry, but glad because our comrades had thought that we had committed suicide, which was not unknown, or deserted, which was also attempted frequently, usually without success.

I have described the clothes we wore for the trip and now we were to see how we fared from leeches that are to be found all over Indochina. Fischer found that his legs and feet were absolutely streaming with blood from the dozen or so leeches that had managed to find their way through his breeches, puttees, socks and boots, whereas I had a couple on my bare feet and only a few spots of blood. The leeches were soon despatched with the aid of the burning end of a cigarette and the risk of infection lessened by the application of saliva on the end of a finger. To drag a leech off one's flesh is a sure way of getting serious infection. I have always been fond of salt on my food and I attribute the lack of interest shown by insects to my body, to the salt in my blood, but I should not tempt Providence by talking about it.

Life at the Academy was very interesting, for the cadets came from a variety of backgrounds. Those from St Cyr were usually from very good families and universities, often with military ancestors; those from St Maixent were primarily NCOs who, according to their superiors were officer material; Poitiers was the school for those with hopes of a future in the Artillery. Young officers and cadets from the Air Force also attended the Academy for certain aspects of their training. I found that among the officers and cadets there were those who were distinctly in favour of the British and de Gaulle, and others who sat on the fence. The former were usually those who became my pupils and the others began to learn German with CSM Driesch.

When I had time, I would march the three or four miles from the Mehl Barracks in Tong to the Academy (which was actually at Sontay), but on most occasions I would take a *pousse-pousse*. I always felt sorry for the boy pulling the two-wheeled fragile-looking vehicle with its long shafts, but they did not seem to mind the job. They always seemed to have money for cigarettes which they rolled themselves and the majority of them appeared to have the mien and the smell of opium addicts. This had always been the weakness of the natives and Ho Chi Minh, who was to be the President of the country after the departure of the French, did his best to outlaw the use of drugs. I am reminded of the fact that many of them, and indeed many of the older native women, had black-lacquered teeth which I was told was something handed down from when the Chinese ruled the country. There is very little difference, to European eyes, in appearance between the Annamese and the pure Chinese person and so to make sure that there was no confusion, the former were obliged to blacken their teeth. The practice was rapidly dying out in my day and people who have been there since tell me that they have never seen anyone with black teeth.

Whilst working at the Academy I would occasionally hear rumblings of discontent which I passed on to the Battalion Intelligence Officer and one or two members of the Battalion were also heard to voice Communist opinions without too much notice being taken. Later on, according to Pierre Sergent's book *The Remarkable Monsieur Frey*, Ernst Frey was reputed to have started a Communist cell at Vietri. I am sure that it was not really a cell but rather four or five intelligent characters who had joined the Legion for the duration of the war and who had been anti-capitalist in civilian life in Europe, who discussed Communism and Socialism just to pass the time. They surely had a 'chip on their shoulder', if you like, and it is also a fact that they were never cut out to be soldiers of France. Yet Frey, Schroeder and Borchers having been liberated as soon as the Second World War ended, were to become Colonels in the Viet Army that was to sweep France from Indochina in 1954. When he returned to East Germany, Borchers became the Head of East German Radio and Schroeder the Editor of an East German newspaper. Frey returned to his native Austria via Siberia and Moscow, then in Vienna, was eventually to become one of the more important members of Catholic society. His adventures were later recounted to Pierre Sergent, a personal friend of my wife and me, leading to the publication of *L'Etrange Monsieur Frey* in 1982, which I have translated into English. Frey's daughter contacted me when her father died (February 1994) and I informed the Foreign Legion so that they can put their records straight. When Frey joined the Viet Army and became military adviser to General Vo Nguyen Giap, leader of the Viet Minh forces and future Vice-President of Viet-Namh, the Indochinese Communist newspaper *Le Peuple,* printed, edited and published by Frey's ex-Legion colleagues, Schroeder and Borchers, in order to prevent probable French persecution, in March 1946 declared that he had died on 8th June 1945. The French repeated the declaration in Frey's military records. To all intents and purposes, in France, he was dead. So, when Frey went to Paris to publicise his book, the authorities could not pursue him through the Courts for treason, though the Press gave the matter much publicity. The Colonel in charge of the Legion Magazine wrote to thank me for the information and assured me that there would be no mention of the 're-decease' in the *Képi Blanc.*

Whilst I was working at the Academy a small resistance movement against the Japanese was formed and I became a member. It must be noted that not all the officers there were with us, and there were only a handful that came from the Legion. The group was organised by Major Carbonel who commanded the Academy but the official orders came from General Mordant, who commanded all the French troops in Indochina. My direct chief was Captain Guy de Cockborne, the 2nd Battalion Commander, later General and French Military Attaché in Korea and still my very good friend. One day I was informed that he wished to see me in his office, purportedly to ask me about my work at the Military Academy. I entered his office and found he was alone. I saluted and removed my *calot* (forage cap) and remained at attention. He told me to stand easy. I noticed that there was a revolver on his desk in front of him. He placed his hand on the weapon and looking me straight in the eyes he said, "Murray, if ever one word of what I am about to say to you gets out to anybody, and I mean *anybody*, I shall personally take great pleasure in putting a bullet through your brain."

"Yes Sir!" I said, "I understand."

Then he told me about the Resistance Movement and its members. There were in fact only four of us from the Legion – Orloff, a Russian; Lalanne, French; Marciniak, French but from a Polish family; Pyl, my Austrian friend who was the PT Instructor, and myself. Pyl was to remain a friend for the rest of his life.

Finally, I felt that I was getting in on the war action and helping the side I wanted to help. Each week we would receive a certain codeword from varied sources and we knew that we had to be at a certain point at a certain time on a certain day. It was always at night when the moon was expected to be bright enough to see parachutes dropping through the night sky and meant that by hook or by crook we had to be where we were expected to be. A lorry would be waiting for us and we would be driven, together with other members of the group from the Colonial Infantry or the Artillery, all sworn to secrecy, and who were also stationed at Tong, to the Dropping Zone out in the wilds. There we would find, or wait for, two or three other lorries from the Academy. The vehicles would be parked off the road and camouflaged, for we never knew when Japanese patrols would come along.

We were all armed with Sten guns which would remain with the lorries after the night's work was completed and we returned to our respective quarters. Eventually the droning sound of a low-flying plane's engines would be heard and we would go to our respective positions; some to watch the approaches, some to light torches and some just to wait to collect the canisters containing arms, ammunition and medical supplies. Soon dark objects would be seen falling while the noise of the plane gradually disappeared. Then all except the guards to the approaches would dash towards the 12ft long canisters that were at least two feet in diameter and very heavy requiring four of us to each one. An officer would keep tally as they were loaded into the lorries and when they had all been found we would join our designated vehicles to escort the material to Hanoi, there to be hidden in the Citadel. Then back to our barracks. Few of the canisters fell outside the zone, but it did happen and then we could not spend too much time looking for them for the Japanese were not deaf, and there were a lot of them about. Only on three occasions do I remember us having to fight our way out through patrols.

One night when I got back to barracks in a very filthy state, for some of the canisters had fallen in a very wet and muddy paddy-field, I found the place in a real state of activity with trenches dug facing the entrance and heavy machine-guns and even a 25mm Oerlikon cannon being positioned. I got over the wall at one of the usual places and went to my room where I was stopped by another Sergeant who informed me that Captain Guillaume wanted me in his office immediately. I said that I would wash first and join the Captain within minutes. 'Not on' the Sergeant told me, he wanted to see me right away, as I was.

My opinion was that Captain Guillaume was not really against the Allies but was pro-Pétain and Vichy and I'm sure he suspected Pyl and myself of being in the Resistance but he himself was naturally, by de Cockborne's express orders, kept uninformed of our activities. He waited for me in his office and furiously demanded where I had been to get into such a state. I told him that I had been drinking a bit and had fallen into a paddy-field on the way back to barracks. I apologised for my appearance but had not had the time to do anything about it. He wanted to know the truth, he shouted, what had I been doing all night? It was now about 4am. I replied that I had been with my concubine, as usual, and that I had a permit to stay out. There was no way that I was going to inform him of the *parachutage* that had taken place at midnight. The revolver of de Cockborne loomed very much in my thoughts.

He declared that he was not satisfied, he knew that I had been out receiving arms and ammunition and the Battalion Commander, de Cockborne, had been with me. I laughed cynically but he said that the information had come from Captain Courant, another Pétainist. Why did I not trust him? He was my Company Commander and could look after me. I stuck to my story and eventually he gave up and told me that I was confined to barracks for the four days that remained of the week until and including Sunday. But every evening there was Cô Thi at the gate with my roast chicken, salad and rice wine.

A few days later I found out that an American plane, carrying out a bombing mission on Japanese installations, had been shot down and the pilot had come down by parachute. The Japanese were out looking for him but friendly natives had rescued him from the paddy-fields and informed a Legion patrol that was also searching for him. He was soon in a prison cell in the Legion barracks and de Cockborne and I visited him the following morning. Two or three days later he was on his way to the Legion 7th Company at Mount Bavi to be shepherded over the border to friendly forces in Chang Kai Chek's China. However, he was still there when the Japanese attacked us on 8th March 1945 and I was never able to find out what happened to him afterwards.

8
The Great Retreat

The Great Retreat actually began on 8th March 1945. I was playing bridge with Marciniak, Garcia and Korst and was winning – the grand sum of about twenty piastres. At 10.15pm the bugle sounded the *Générale* which I had first heard in Sidi-bel-Abbès when war broke out, over five years previously. Dropping the cards on the table, I told the others that we must hurry to get into *tenue de campagne*, collect our rifles and fall in outside Battalion HQ. They trusted me and did as I suggested, telling everybody we met what was to be done. Members of the Guard were also shouting out orders. Orderly chaos resulted and soon the whole battalion was formed up and ready to go to war.

At midnight, the combined forces of the Legion, Colonial Artillery and Colonial Infantry, some 2,000 strong though very poorly armed, marched out of Tong under the direction of General Alessandri. In order to avoid a massacre of the European population, composed almost exclusively of the families of his soldiers, Alessandri marched the troops out of Tong so the town could be declared *ville ouverte* (an open city). The General intended to fight the enemy in the hills and mountains and along the narrowest paths he could find; the most difficult terrain for the enemy to follow. He knew that, unlike the Japanese, he would be unable to receive fresh supplies of troops, arms and ammunition, unless by parachute from the Americans, so he would make it as difficult as possible for them by keeping as far from the roads as practicable. He had left behind in Tong, to look after the needs of the civilian population, of invalids and office staff, Lieutenant-Colonel Marcelin who had been the officer in charge of the garrison for a number of years. He was a well-loved, staunch, long-serving Legion officer with a recently-married son, an officer in the Regiment. Lieutenant-Colonel Marcelin spent the night of the 9th March 1945 in his office on the first floor of his garrison block just over the road from the Legion guardroom. He had assembled his numerous secretaries and messengers on the ground floor.

Much later, when I was in Calcutta, I received a note from Mme Korst, wife of a Regimental Sergeant-Major of the Paymaster's Office, apologising for having used a brand-new cream summer suit that I had left in my wardrobe at Tong, to make clothes for her children. "I know that you would have given it to me, had you been there" and how right she was, for the internees were to suffer much privation during the months to come. We later found out the full story of what happened at Tong after our departure and it was horrific.

On the 10th March, at about 6.30 am, the Japanese, screaming like maniacs to frighten the adversary, erupted into the garrison where only non-combatants were to be found. One group dashed into the Supplies Depot bayoneting to death all the personnel in the bakery. The next day some of them were even found dead still clutching the dough they had been kneading for the daily bread. Another group raced at the double with the bayonets on their rifles pointing to the sky and with grenades in their hands towards the garrison offices. Personnel on the ground floor were literally blown to pieces by the grenades as they were hurled through doors and windows and those who did not die from the bombs were finished off with bayonets. Not one person managed to escape the awful slaughter.

Meanwhile a party of perhaps ten Japanese rushed into the Colonel's office firing pistol bullets into him before trying to kill him with their bayonets. He was left there, bleeding to death, to expire on the 11th, but not before calling to his side several NCOs and instructing them to do everything possible to ensure the wellbeing of the women and children who would all now be interned in the Legion barracks.

❧

On leaving Tong, we had in front of us, as part of my Company, an old Renault tank of the 1914–18 war. Its weaponry consisted of an ancient Hotchkiss machine-gun and some sort of old cannon. It stayed with us, never firing a single round, for about five miles and then was discarded in the middle of the Black River when we came to cross it, together with a great amount of our mortars and ammunition lost from the backs of mules as they swam across. There was panic, and I am not ashamed to say that I felt it too, because the enemy were in sight in armoured cars behind us and this was a new experience for many of us. We were joined at Kim Day, some three or four miles from Tong, by some of the airmen who were to render such great service during the succeeding weeks. They had no planes but they proved very courageous companions even on foot.

On the 12th March, Captain Courant, who had been in Bavi with the 7th Company, joined us. He had been heliographed by Lt Col Marcelin with updates on Tong. The camp on Mount Bavi was still under construction and the telephone had not yet been installed. The only means of communication was by horse or motorcycle courier, both of which took time, or by heliograph which required sunshine, but was much quicker. Unfortunately, the 7th had then been surrounded by the enemy and had to fight their way out of a most difficult situation and then lost almost all of their war material when they crossed the Black River to escape. They were in much the same situation as us.

On the following day, Captain Courant, who had taken over the CA2 from Guillaume, came and handed me a large bundle of what looked like bedsheets. They were in fact signalling panels. He reported that we were expecting assistance from American planes and I was to remain behind the whole column, armed with just my new Remington rifle, several chargers for it and a few hand grenades. The rifle had been dropped by American planes, together with some British army boots. I was one of the very few who could wear the boots without cutting chunks out of the leather.

I used the panels on four occasions; for these were the only times when we were helped by the Americans and their twin-fuselaged Black Widows. I remember the first time so plainly as the Japanese were only about four hundred yards behind us and really in force at this point. Captain Courant, before hurrying on with our company, told me to signal this fact to the Americans as they flashed past only hundreds of feet above us. I quickly stretched out my panels telling them where the enemy was and minutes after, screaming round in the smallest possible circle, the two planes came back and dropped clusters of bombs on the enemy. I grabbed up my panels and dashed after the company to report that I had observed direct hits on the Japanese and when last seen, they were scattering in all directions.

At the next village, I discovered from the chief that there was a Japanese ammunition dump quite nearby and, through hand signs, he indicated to me its exact location. I informed Captain Courant, who was suitably impressed, and when the Black Widows returned about an hour later, I laid out my 'bedsheets' once again to give them the relevant coordinates of the dump. Within minutes there was a terrific explosion as the dump went up in smoke and flames and was no longer. The other two occasions were similarly successful; holes were blown in the metalled road, not only making the Japanese disappear into the forest on either side of it but also preventing, or at least delaying, the use of the road by their lorries with new troops and victuals, etc.

Shortly after these successes, I was told to destroy the signalling panels as we were not going to receive any more help from the Americans. The terrain that we were about to enter was not suitable for aerial intervention. Thick forests, narrow, rocky paths along the rivers, through the mountains and over passes of between 5,000 and 8,000 feet high; in short it was terrain that would test us to our limits.

Shortly after I had burned my signalling panels, Captain Courant called Sergeant Dalzotto and myself. He had been ordered to destroy the bridge we had crossed an hour past and he was now ordering the two of us to do the dirty work. Ours was not to reason why. We could not reasonably expect him to do it and refusing the order would have given him the opportunity to shoot us. So, we collected the necessary gelignite, fuses and detonators from a case carried on a mule, slung our rifles across our shoulders, and marched back through our advancing forces to the bridge. We fixed the charges under the old construction with about six feet of fuse and then we waited until all our troops had passed, plus another half hour to allow for stragglers. But all of a sudden, we saw enemy troops running towards us. There was no time to lose. We set light to the shortened fuses and ran for it. Seconds later there was a tremendous crash and we knew the bridge had gone. It would take some hours for the enemy to find another way of fording the river which was quite wide and very deep at that point. After marching at the double for several hours, we caught up with our company now on rear guard.

After a few more miles, the company in front of us halted to cover the column and we went past them to new positions, overtaking the companies in front, until we were in the van with our own *éclaireurs* facing left and right and ahead to recce for signs of the Japanese. The rest of the section digging in, in a manner of speaking, facing the enemy while the other companies marched past us. This was the way we retreated, on and on and on. By destroying the signalling panels, my responsibility to stay back to send messages was gone and I was now free to return to my company. I turned my attentions to giving assistance to those soldiers who were not able to keep up with the main body because of sore feet, beriberi, or fatigue. But there was only so much I, or anyone, could do to help them and at certain points, we had to leave them behind to look after themselves. I know that many of them perished in the forests through hunger or from attacks by wild beasts or were killed by the Japanese to whom they tried to surrender. It was a terrible time.

Shortly after the bridge incident, Captain Courant came to inform me that I was now in charge of my section and that if I carried on as I had been doing, I would be sent to OTC (Officer Training) as soon as it was possible. I never could fathom out Courant: one minute he would be showing me that he hated my guts, and now here he was promoting me under fire.

When we were just about a week's march from the Chinese frontier at Lao-Kay, an ancient Potez 25 plane flew over and a length of bamboo was thrown out of the cockpit. It contained orders from General Sabattier, General Alessandri's superior, to turn south-west towards Son La where a concentration of enemy troops under Colonel Tojoé was reportedly making its way towards the Legion position. We marched three hundred and fifty kilometres in three days, along tarmacked roads that burned our blistered feet, and through dense, humid jungles where leeches clung to exposed flesh. They even managed to get through puttees and stockings and down into the boots that some of us still wore. We crossed over raging torrents and stopped at pleasant streams where we were able to drink our fill, but still with the ever-present possibility of ambushes by the Japanese. But we got there, at last, to Son La.

The village of Son La is on the Black River and a strong point had been constructed there in late 1941 by sixty légionnaires and sixty native troops under the command of Lieut Chenel. Out in the wilderness it was essential that the CO had absolute confidence in each and every soldier. Very harsh treatment was certainly required on occasions and *le tombeau* would be ordered, even though it was against the rules. I think it was only ever used as a punishment out in North Africa and Indochina. The trouble-maker had to dig a hole in the ground, in the sun, just the right size for him to lie down, covered by a groundsheet, or occasionally barbed-wire. One day and a night in the 'grave' was enough to bring the most recalcitrant of offenders to their senses. This may well seem inhumane today and I suppose it was, but it certainly adhered to the theory of 'rough justice' and prepared légionnaires well for warfare and conflict.

Just a few hours after reaching Son La we faced thousands of Japanese troops. This was the real thing and all Hell broke loose, mostly in dense forest. As we had troops detailed to watch the flanks, we knew that anything that moved in front of us was the enemy. It was difficult for either side to use mortars because of overhanging branches that could interfere with the shells and could be of more danger to the sender than the proposed receiver. It was hand-to-hand fighting with rifles, revolvers and eventually bayonets. It was horrendous and for many years after I used to wake up in the night hearing the out-of-this-world screams of the Nippons as they attacked, together with the awful cries of our own wounded and dying.

At one point in this odious battle, I heard a sharp cry and on looking around I saw the 1st class soldier Nocke fall to the ground. I crawled to him and found that he had been shot in the upper leg. I took off his belt and quickly made a tourniquet above the wound as it was bleeding heavily. I dragged him back to the rear where I managed to find a mule without its charge of heavy machine gun and ammunition. With the assistance of Lieutenant Pepin-Lehalleur I got Nocke on to the back of the mule where he was able to grab the reins to hold himself on. Facing the animal in the right direction I gave it a hard slap on its rear end and off it trotted. Pepin-Lehalleur had been my officer instructor at Saïda, in Algeria, and I held him in great respect. I never met Nocke again but I heard that he was eventually evacuated by plane from Dien-bien-Phu with Captain de Cockborne who had also been wounded, and received treatment in Pondichéry, near Calcutta in India.

After three hours of heavy fighting, the General, fearing that we were about to be encircled completely, ordered the retreat. We had lost fifty-eight légionnaires and two officers at Son La, but the Japanese lost several hundred men.

As we continued our retreat towards the frontier, crossing a bare plain with foothills to right and left, I marched along, fifty yards or so behind my scouts, dragging my weary feet. My eyes were very tired but I still kept an alert lookout. Suddenly I heard the thunder of hooves approaching from behind and dropped quickly to the ground, my rifle ready to fire, but I recognised a friend; it was Captain Komaroff. We had been stationed in Sidi-bel-Abbès together and had enjoyed many a conversation in English, in which he was quite fluent. He drew up beside me and offered me a couple of packs of American cigarettes. "I don't smoke cigarettes, sir," I said, "but I can easily put them in my pipe." He bent down from the saddle to hand them to me and as I took them there came a strange thud and an awful red stain appeared on his forehead. He made no sound and I knew that he was dead. I grabbed at him as he began to slide towards me and held him up as I called out for help. Sergent Monch, also of Battalion HQ, ran towards me and held the Captain up on the other side, while another soldier took the reins of the horse and led him rapidly forward towards Battalion Headquarters. During the hours that followed most of the Battalion marched past the body of Captain Komaroff to salute a brave soldier and good friend, before he was taken on to be buried at Dien-bien-Phu. The general impression and future reports of his death indicated that he was killed by a piece of shrapnel, for mortar bombs were occasionally exploding round us at the time, but I was there with him and I know that it was from the bullet of a sniper in the foothills some hundred yards away. But, of course, it is quite academic. Our friend Komaroff was gone, and the method of his going could change nothing at all.

We then came to the Pass of the Méos where our route wound up and round the mountainside to the very top before twisting its way down to the plain of Dien-Bien-Phu and Phong Saly where strong points were to be established. By now, our manoeuvres were well-rehearsed. The leading section would wait in the ditch beside the mountain wall that formed promontories as the road bent in and out until every other section had passed. Then the light machine gun would be set up in the shallow ditch with the other men crouching low with their rifles and they would all fire at the enemy as soon as they poked their noses round the preceding bend. When the enemy retreated, the section would retire to the head of the column while the next section would lie in wait for the enemy. It was during the time that my section was waiting for the enemy along the *Col des Méos,* that I suddenly realised that a clump of bamboos on the other side of the road probably indicated the cliff there was not so abrupt as it was in other places. I slid quickly across the road and indeed there was access, howsoever precarious, to the road below and on that road were a dozen Japanese creeping cautiously upwards. The Japanese troops wore canvas boots that were like mittens with one compartment, if I may call it that, for the big toe and another for the rest of the toes. These allowed them to scale trees and precipitous cliffs with the agility of monkeys. Now here they were about fifty yards away, below me. I rapidly drew the pins from my last two grenades, waited three or four seconds and threw them into the group. They had started firing at me as soon as I had stuck my head over the top. Then came two explosions and I risked a peep. There was no movement from down there, but there was from behind me as the Japanese appeared round the bend to be met by the fire from my section. The enemy disappeared and we retired in good order to the front of the detachment.

It was decided that Dien Bien Phu was not such a good place to set up a defensive position as there were so many small routes that led there and what's more the Japanese were already in possession of the airfield not far from the town. The small Colonial and native detachment on duty there had sold their lives most dearly. We passed through without stopping but not before I went into the hospital that had been emptied, pillaged and evacuated. I found a bag of sucrose, about 2lbs I suppose, which served my section well during the days to come. In French it is called *système 'D'*; the English equivalent I suppose is looking after, number one/one's own. We also paid our respects at the graves of Captain Komaroff, Lance-Sergeant Kolerski, Corporal Fenelli and Company Sergeant-Major Diehl. So many great men had been lost.

On Sunday 8th April, we made temporary camp on the edge of a stream that was probably a tributary of the Nam Ou. It was a lovely day and we were at rest, as much as we could be. Other units were protecting our flanks so the members of my section were able to enjoy a quick meal of rice and pork that had turned up out of nowhere – *système 'D'* again I suppose. Sentries were posted and the rest of us stripped to the waist and went to the babbling stream. I had left Lance-Sergeant Argaud and two légionnaires behind to guard the stacked rifles, including my new Remington repeater that I had been given by the General himself. It was light and I was very proud of it. I caressed it tenderly as I leaned it, loaded, due to the circumstances, beside a tree, telling Argaud not to touch it nor to allow anyone else to touch it. I had just dipped my head and shoulders into the water when suddenly there was the report of a gun. I stood up and turned around in time to see Légionnaire Kuhn, who had just joined us a few hours before, fall to the ground. Dashing across I lifted his head and saw nothing amiss, until I turned him over and saw that a bullet had traversed his back, entering the fleshy part of his shoulder, exiting near his spine, only to re-enter the fleshy part of the other shoulder, leaving four bleeding flesh wounds. Calling for emergency packs, I raised his shoulders and with assistance, managed to do quite a good job on the wounds, staunching the flow of blood. It was a miracle that the bullet had not touched his spine, a matter of the thickness of a cigarette paper away. But Kuhn was in pain and could not rise so we made a stretcher out of bamboo, a ground sheet and leather straps, and placed him in the shade. I asked Argaud what had happened for it had become evident from what the men were saying that the bullet had come from my own Remington.

Argaud confessed that he had picked my rifle up to look at it as it was the first time he had occasion to examine such a gun; his finger had slipped on to the trigger and the shot had been fired. I felt like kicking his behind into kingdom come, but just then Lieutenant Desfossés arrived and said that the matter would be discussed later, the enemy was in sight. I asked him what we should do with Kuhn as we couldn't just leave him there. The Lieutenant said that as it was my section that was responsible, one of my groups should now pick him up on the stretcher and carry him down the mountainside to the village of Pak Ban on the River Nam Ou. As head of section I felt responsible and that I should do my part to help. We were to transport him down-river to the next village in a dug-out canoe where we would land and wait for the battalion. The descent of the mountain path was horrendous; there were only eight of us in the group so we had to change over every fifteen minutes, so heavy was the going. We finally made it to the village and found sufficient *pirogues* to take us all, with the stretcher, and quite a number of other ill and wounded. We floundered somehow down to the next village of Huong Hong and managed to land and gain the main road where there was a *camion* to transport those unable to rejoin the column. Where it went to I never had the time to find out. Kuhn was able to stand, and even to walk, now that the shock of the accident had worn off, although somehow I think that the rough handling he had received had been the best medicine. We rejoined our company a few hours afterwards and all was back to normal. I would have dealt with Argaud later but there was just not the time for, within minutes of our rejoining the company, the enemy was upon us again.

It was just around this time that my old Hungarian friend, Sergeant Svoboda, who had one day sworn to me that he would never be taken alive by the Japanese, was captured by the enemy while he was out reconnoitring. He was in a very poor state but had volunteered for the job. I learned from him later that his captors had given him a load that he found too heavy to carry and he began to lag behind. He was taken into the woods by a Japanese officer who fired several rounds from his revolver into him and left him for dead. He survived the murderous attack and eventually struggled towards the river that he could hear some distance away. He fainted on the way and when he came to he found himself in a native hut to which he had been dragged by a young Laotian woman who looked after him until he could leave by boat. He was apparently taken to a village downstream, then on horseback and sometimes carried on a stretcher, by relay, and eventually arrived in China. I was never able to find out how he reached India, for when I saw him in the French Hospital at Chandernagore (then a French possession but the people there opted for inclusion in the State of India in July 1949), he was still in a very poor state, but he was alive. The distances travelled and journeys made by the wounded on all sides of the global conflict were quite staggering.

On the 18th April, my Company, the 7th of the 2nd Battalion, was ordered to stop in a reasonably-sized village where we purchased a suckling pig and a few chickens. Had the head of the village not accepted the amount of money offered by Captain Courant, it is certain that we would have taken them anyhow. The pig was slaughtered and the birds plucked and readied for the barbecue. A wood fire was begun but as it had been raining cats and dogs it was not very successful until some idiot found a can of paraffin and poured most of it on to the small flames. There was only a moment of smoke and then the fire really began to take hold. Up and up went the flames, only to be caught by a sudden gust of wind that blew them on to a nearby thatched roof. Within less time than it takes to tell the story, the

The Musique at a village called Miliani
(Author's Collection)

The Empire Theatre, Sidi-bel-Abbes,
Maurice Chevalier
(Author's Collection)

The French Foreign Legion Monument at Sidi-bel-Abbes (now relocated at Aubagne)
(Author's Collection)

CARBINE
MOD. 1916

MARCHING KIT
1941 - 1965
INDO - CHINA
5TH REGIMENT.

EM.

Marching Kit, French Foreign Legion,
Indochina, 1941–1945
(Author's Collection)

Caricature of Murray drawn by L. Chanson
(Author's Collection)

Camerone celebration Tong 1939
(Andrew J Mitchell)

Legionnaires celebrating
(Andrew J Mitchell)

de Cockborne, Bjerring and Marcelin 1941
(Andrew J Mitchell)

Marcelin Camerone 1941
(Andrew J Mitchell)

5e REI March to border
(Andrew J Mitchell)

*5e REI China June
1945 proper*
(Andrew J Mitchell)

China – "delousing expedition"
(Author's Collection)

China – "group of Chinese Guerillas"
(Author's Collection)

China – "restaurant in Yunnan Province"
(Author's Collection)

China – "traders en route to town to sell wool, tobacco and rice"
(Author's Collection)

Murray in India 1945
(Author's Collection)

Camerone Day, Aubagne, 1987
(Author's Collection)

whole village went up in flames. How the innocents suffer in war! Luckily the head of the village had sent his people with what remained of their stock and possessions into the hills before joining them himself after receiving our payment. There was no loss of life and we even managed to save the few mules we had left, our arms and most of our reserve ammunition. The most remarkable thing was that, apart from ashes and a few metal pots remaining after the conflagration, a great stone Buddha that had stood in the middle of the village, still stood there, just a little blackened by the smoke, looking proud, untouchable and dignified. The sight of it still remains with me to this day, and it is most humbling in a mysterious way.

Our next strong point was fixed at Phong Saly whence all the inhabitants had fled taking with them everything of any value or use to us. My friend, Pyl, myself and two others were sent off to find out what we could about the enemy. As we rested for a moment on a high point, keeping our heads down as we surveyed the countryside, we suddenly heard the roar of an aeroplane motor and a small plane was seen coming towards us. We prepared to make our presence known for it looked like our Potez 25 that had been used by the General to transmit orders, but suddenly we saw that it bore the red setting sun of Japan on the side and we all ducked. The pilot had not been sleeping; he had seen movement and *rat...tat...tat* went his machine-guns. Stony chips spattered us as we lay motionless, sheltered by the rocks behind which we lay. I was in agony for as I had darted for shelter my foot had been caught between two boulders and my ankle was sprained. The plane disappeared and we returned to our unit to report that we had seen no signs of ground forces. Here we were joined by some members of the 3rd Battalion who had been cut off from the main body of their battalion on our left flank. They had found it easier to fight their way towards us rather than towards the 3rd. They were in a terrible state, having not eaten for days but we were all in the same boat, and they were very glad to be with us. The beauty of carrying on along the bank of the River Nam Ou which was quite wide, was that it restricted the approach of the enemy from behind for they were constrained as we were, to keep in single file, and their front men kept getting it from our rear-guard, slowly retreating and being replaced at frequent intervals.

My sprained ankle made it very hard for me to keep up but eventually I was able to dispense with the stick I had been using. It is amazing how much pain one can support when sudden death is stalking you just a few hundred yards behind. But, of course, I was not the only one staggering on, in fact we were all suffering from some sort of ailment and hope was almost gone. We were definitely not Christian soldiers, but we kept marching on and John Bunyan's Christian was often in my thoughts, when I was not on rear-guard for then I was filled with very un-Christian thoughts *vis-à-vis* the Japanese. My own company, once more than a hundred, was now reduced to sixty or so and other companies were in the same parlous condition; so many friends gone; dead, wounded, left behind because they were unable to continue, taken prisoner.

The other factor that carried great influence on the way a battle could go, or how our mood could be, was the weather. There were days and nights that were beautiful up in the mountains and down in the valleys were it not for the continuous vigil we had to keep for the enemy, but there were times when the skies just opened to pour down on us those torrents of rain that one only sees in tropical countries. Oh of course we see downpours in our European countries; multiply the worst of them three times or more and one can then imagine the immensity of the absolute sheets of water drenching everything in the East, changing a dusty road or terrain into a river of inches deep sticky sludge or an almost impassable steaming lake. Since the destruction of the village by fire we had been ordered never to use native accommodation as shelter, even though we no longer had tents or waterproof sheets, to avoid the risk of antagonising the mountain peoples further. The General was still convinced that France would return to Indochina.

On the 19th April, we had such a downpour which lasted for several hours and radio contact was entirely lost. For days it had been very difficult to keep in touch with the 3rd Battalion on our left flank and we had to rely on the information given by those few poor souls who had been separated from the main battalion during their numerous encounters with the enemy. We arrived at Phong Saly on the 23rd April, and dug in. The 2nd Battalion had to hold the fort for as long as possible to allow as much of the whole column, separated units and isolated soldiers to pass us and make their way towards the frontier, one hundred and thirty miles or so away to the north and north-west, through very mountainous country.

Major Carbonel, my friend from the Academy who was in charge of our part of the column, received news that the Japanese forces were level with us to the east and there was the distinct possibility that they would make their way west to cut off our retreat to the frontier, twenty miles or so after Ma Li Tao. Something had to be done. Captain de Cockborne, commanding the 2nd Battalion, ordered my Section of the 7th Company to remain dug in at Phong Saly, facing the Japanese in the east. We stayed there without food or rest for twenty-four hours and then rejoined the main force, having to fight our way through several Japanese groups before doing so and then continued our route towards the frontier.

For the first two days the road was quite easy, though we had been joined by numerous sick and wounded and had to move at their rate of progress which was dead slow. They did their best to get in front of the column but it was too much to expect. We had no radio communication with other troops and it was now very difficult to find the best ways to go for our Laotian interpreter could neither understand, nor make himself understood, by the Ho, Lu and Kha natives we met in the mountains. The path that we followed, one of the many options chosen by Carbonel, took us through narrow, misty passes more than five thousand feet above sea level, having been told by the guides we now had, that lower paths were too narrow and dangerous for the few horses that we had left.

We finally reached this last main village before the frontier during the afternoon of the 30th April 1945. It is a date that has particular resonance with all Légionnaires as it was when one of the Legion's most heroic battles took place in Camerone, Mexico. But we could not celebrate for not only did we not have any strong liquor but we were also far from being in any kind of celebratory mood. We still had many miles to go before we could consider ourselves safe from the Japanese. The village was positioned in dense forest and the job of the 1st and 2nd Battalions was to prevent the Japanese from cutting the road to the frontier. The 7th Company got to the village at about 4pm and installed itself in a defensive position facing east and south-east. We felt, rather than saw, the enemy gathering round us. It was a strange and ominous time.

Finally, at about 6am, on 1st May, the attack came, preceded by mortar shells, one of the first of which fell on de Cockborne's command post, killing several horses and wounding several légionnaires.

Minutes later, Hell broke loose and the screaming horde of Nippons came crashing through the trees. Captain de Cockborne was wounded in the arm and separated from his equine friend, Estafette, for a while until she came pounding back towards him together with another mare. It was as if she knew that the frontier was not too far away and the Japanese were not going to stop her getting there after all the suffering and poor rations she had been receiving for so many weeks. Estafette was eventually to die months later in China, but for many years General de Cockborne had a 'double' of the strawberry mare living a life of ease and luxury on his estate near Troyes in eastern France, just to remind him of his old friend.

However, back at Ma Li Tao the battle raged with the enemy pounding our positions with mortars and heavy machine-gun fire. Sergeant Kabilik and

Légionnaire Wassovitch were wounded within my reach, while Légionnaires Molinello, Feihs and Mencassola were to disappear, presumed killed. Just before we retired I saw one of the cadets from the Academy appear in the doorway of a hut that he had apparently been searching, some 20 yards away, and was met with a hail of bullets from the hidden enemy. His chest was just a gaping hole and I could see that he was dead before he reached the ground.

The enemy seemed to be behind every tree in the vicinity and bullets, many of them tracers, were streaming round us while cries of 'Banzai! Banzai!' came from the advancing hordes. Then the whistles went and orders were shouted for us to retire as arranged along the road to Khau Phya and Muong Le while other units took the road to Ou Neua.

During those awful times, the movement from life to death became almost banal. The sense of decency of men accepting death for a just cause was one of the most touching things I found as we fought those dreadful battles. The majority of the légionnaires seemed to sense when a battle was to be fought and prepared themselves for life or death by cleaning themselves up as well as they could in the circumstances. Whenever the opportunity presented itself, they shaved and washed, and scraped dried mud from their clothing and even their boots or whatever they had to cover their broken feet. Were they preparing to meet their Maker, or friends and colleagues who had passed on before them? Perhaps it was just Legion discipline that made it essential that they do so before *la sortie en ville?* I did it myself yet I could not provide an answer for my motives, except perhaps that I was somehow able to see much more clearly in those hours or even minutes before battle, than I normally could see. Was it that we just wanted to face death with dignity, like the ancient Greek and Roman heroes: '...eat, drink, be merry...' (and as clean as possible)... '...for tomorrow you may die'? I know that when my own section was not engaged, I envied those that were, and it was plain that my colleagues were of the same mind. How often looking at those who had been killed, I was amazed at the peace and serenity upon their faces, and I think that this sort of prepared me for possible, nay probable, death on the field of battle. 'If I should die, think only this of me...' How often did I recite to myself those words of Rupert Brooke, the famous poet who was to die at Gallipoli, on a foreign field, on 23rd April 1915?

By the time we reached China, the Alessandri Column had marched over a thousand miles and fought sixteen battles with an enemy at least ten times its number. They had followed us relentlessly, with continually refreshed troops, materials and victuals. We, on the other hand, were always very hungry, thirsty, fatigued and often with little hope. But the Legion carried on regardless, ever ready to fight, ever inspiring other detachments to drag their weary feet on and on, encouraged throughout by magnificent officers, supported by *les maréchaux* of which I am proud to have been one. We fought an enemy prepared to sink to the very depths of bestiality, but the Legion lived up to its renown and I am proud to say that I was there. Of the 350 légionnaires of the 2nd Battalion who had left Tong, only 243 arrived in China for there had been: 46 killed, 26 wounded and evacuated, 15 disappeared (taken prisoner and killed) and 20 evacuated sick. Of my own 7th Company, numbering 70 after the escape from Bavi, 10 were killed and 12 wounded including one officer; of the 6th Coy: effective 110, one officer and one other killed, 3 wounded; of the 5th Coy: effective 90, one officer and one other killed, 3 wounded and 15 disappeared, presumed dead; of the Support (Heavy weapons) Company: effective 90, one killed, 2 wounded and 15 made prisoner (probably massacred later); while of the Administrative Company: 4 killed, 4 wounded, including two officers, 12 prisoners presumed dead and one légionnaire was to die in China. The other two battalions had suffered similarly.

Shortly after Ma Li Tao General Alessandri issued the following despatch to his troops:

Officers, Non-Commissioned Officers, Corporals and Légionnaires of the 5th Regiment of the Foreign Legion – badly nourished, poorly clad, sadly shod, weary and fatigued by privation and suffering ... you marched on your way and fought without respite with only one thing in mind ... to remain faithful to your posts. I would like you to know that today you have added a most glorious new page to the Golden Book of the Foreign Legion. On this day, the 30th April, 1945, I send you my most sincere sentiments of affection and profound recognition. I render homage to your soldierly virtues and I bow low before your comrades fallen on the Field of Honour and salute the grandeur of their sacrifice.

Signed: ALESSANDRI

9
From China to India and the
End of a Chapter

Most of the 2nd Battalion crossed the frontier after Ma Li Tao between 2nd and 4th May. Captain de Cockborne, in view of the severity of his wounds, had handed his Battalion over to my one-time boss in the Ordnance Office at Vietri, Captain Besset (I was once informed that he was actually a French Count and entitled to use the *de* in front of his name). He also had the 6th Company under his command. A sudden Japanese attack broke the battalion in two forcing the 5th and 6th to follow the Ou Neua road and the 7th, still under Captain Courant, to take the longer route, as planned, via Khau Phia towards Muong Le leaving the enemy behind at last. Once again Captain Courant sprung a surprise on me and ordered me to take one of my groups forward, now only four men, as quickly as I could and try to make some arrangements for food and lodging for the 7th. I have no doubts that I was chosen because I was English and Chiang Kai Chek was favourably disposed towards us.

We were very lucky for after a few miles we met up with a Chinese Major called Wu who had received news of our arrival and had been sent to meet us. He was mounted and accompanied by his batman, also on a horse. We had our rifles slung over our shoulders. I saluted him and he replied. I said, "Bonjour" and he nodded. I said, "Good day, Sir" and his face lit up with a big smile as he replied, "Good day, Sir". I then said that I hoped he spoke English for I was English even though I was a French soldier. He understood everything I said and was quite able to carry on a conversation. I put the Major in the picture and he told me that his General, who was in command of the whole area, had sent him to tell us what we were to do. He would take me and my men to the next place where our Company was to camp, turned his horse to face in the direction we had been travelling and spoke to his batman who got off his horse. The Major told me to mount and we would travel together, but I told him that my men were on foot and therefore I must walk as well. He dismounted and handed the reins of his horse to his colleague and we all marched on together. He was really delighted to speak English and thanked me for coming his way. After an hour or so he said that he must go ahead to arrange things; I must tell my commander to carry on in the same direction and a resting place would be prepared for us with some food for which we must pay. The two of them rode off while I waited for the Captain and the rest of the 7th Company. We continued our march and in the late afternoon we came to a village where the Major was waiting for us. He directed the légionnaires to a field where fires were burning under cooking pots filled with wild rice and chicken bits. There was sufficient for all. It really was the most wonderful sight for our poor, weary men. The Major escorted me to a small hut and we had our meal together while we talked about our battles and the situation in Europe and China. By killing so many Japanese we had done a great thing for China and they were very grateful. He left me to sleep in the hut and also gave me a round, plate-sized lump of sugar as a present.

The next morning, we continued onwards, the Major, his batman and myself with my four men marching ahead of the Company across the Plain of Yunnan towards Pu Erh Fu, a largish town which we were directed to pass around. On the far side of the town, however, he called a halt and told Captain Courant and myself to follow him to a solid white bungalow where we came face to face with the General. We saluted and he nodded his head. He then spoke to Captain Courant; the Major translated for me and I told the Captain what was said. The General was ordering us to lay down all our arms in front of the bungalow for we must carry on, unarmed, to our final destination at Tsao Pa, many miles away to the East. Captain Courant asked me to explain to the General, in the nicest possible way, that we were set on fighting our common enemy, the Japanese, very soon, for the French were all to group at Tsao Pa. Therefore, laying down our arms was out of the question. The discussions required not only my best language skills but diplomacy and negotiation too. We were told to leave the building whilst the two officers stayed inside to discuss the matter. After what felt like a very long time, we were recalled to be told that the General, as a great favour, would allow us to keep our arms, but we must give him as much gold as possible. CSM Korst, our Treasurer, was called in and asked to show how much gold he actually had.

Korst was a German, of Jewish descent I am sure, who had been in the Legion for a good ten years. He felt that this was an occasion when it was more prudent to be truthful as we all felt that the Chinese General was quite capable of turning everything out on the road to look for hidden gold should he not believe Korst. Another diplomatic discussion took place; Korst argued, Captain Courant argued, and I translated to the Major who repeated it all to the General until an arrangement was finally reached. It was very expensive but ultimately everybody was satisfied. I am quite sure somehow that our Treasurer had more gold hidden away somewhere. I learned later that we were the only Company to arrive in China and retain our arms, and I shall always say that it was thanks to my friend Major Wu and me.

During the next few days the Major remained by my side as we made our weary way towards Tsao Pa where we were joined by other detachments of the Alessandri Column as tired, weary and decimated as we were. But we were very relieved that the natives were friendly. I think Major Wu was grateful for his English conversation and every time we approached the village where we were to camp for the night, he would ride ahead to arrange things. This always included, not only a hut for me but, a chunk of heavy sugar which I never failed to distribute to my section as an addition to their diet of wild rice and chicken with the occasional pork. I also managed to obtain local rice liquor sometimes, which of course was most welcome to my men. When we came to the limit of the General's influence, the Major had to leave us and he did so with the minimum of emotion. He had done his job and I believe that he had enjoyed it. We exchanged names and addresses without any hope of communication yet I did write twice from Calcutta and received one short reply, but no more.

We eventually reached the village of Pu Erh Fu and when we stopped to rest a few miles further on, more or less in the middle of a jungle, I took the opportunity to speak with Captain Courant. There was a matter that was pressing on my mind and had been for quite some time. I had come to the end of my eighth year of service in the Legion, and as the Legion was presently out of the fight against the Japanese and the Axis forces, I wished to get to a British or American base as soon as possible. I recounted all this to the Captain, with as much respect and diplomacy as I could muster. He told me that this was against all the rules and regulations and called a meeting of officers to talk about it. General Alessandri arrived. I referred to the last General Order that had appeared in Tong signed by General Mordant, and which I knew that Alessandri had seen and understood. It had actually originated in the French Ministry of Defence and stated more or less that '... any légionnaire coming to the end of his engagement in the Far East (not specifically Indochina) could be released provided the representative of his country of origin was in agreement'. I insisted that the nearest British Consul must be far away and Courant could not possibly disagree. Eventually, General Alessandri and I carried the day. He was my friend. He gave me permission to leave; it was 12th May 1945.

I shook hands with the General and the other officers who were present and then went to say a quick farewell to the men of my section. I stood on a wall with my hand to my forehead in a final salute to those 'men without names' as they waved *en passant*. They knew that they would probably never again see *l'Anglais* with whom they had shared so much. Courant was not very happy and called me a deserter as he marched past. This saddened me somewhat for I knew that I was no deserter. I had given eight years of service to the Legion and never faltered in the line of duty. But my desire to fight for my own nation, and to get at the Japanese as soon as possible was stronger. I knew I had to leave the Legion to do it. I would not let it worry me too much for I knew that Courant would regret the appellation before the day was out and realise that I had served the Legion well.

I returned to Pu Erh Fu to get my bearings. I was made most welcome by the Head of the town and given food and a place to get my head down. I found out that there was 'a *man of God*' in a '*place of God*' not far away. I went there the next day and found a great Dane over six and a half feet tall! He was a missionary serving a vast area that he covered on foot for he could never ride the small ponies of the region; his knees would have trailed on the ground. But he was a lovely man, speaking good English and on the third day there he escorted me to the nearest town where there happened to be a Vice-Consul. He told me that the only way I would get to Kunming and British forces would be via the 14th US Air Force which had a meteorological base some miles away, unless I felt like walking between four and five hundred miles over some of the worst country in the world, through districts overrun by bandits and wild animals.

So, we walked to the base, about four miles away, where I was welcomed by the Lieutenant in command and introduced to the company. They were not numerous for all they had to do was send up huge balloons into the atmosphere and the instruments attached would record information required before they burst at a pre-determined height and a parachute would bring the instruments back to earth where they were collected by the Americans. Some of course went astray, but not often, and the information was vital to Kunming whence planes flew against the enemy forces in South East Asia.

I was looked after by those American friends for over a week; fed and entertained with films every day, and in turn I entertained them with my tales of the Legion and songs of old England which they seemed to enjoy. Several times we were visited by officers and officials from Indochina and also a number of sick or wounded Legion friends, all asking for transport to Kunming for onward transmission to Calcutta. I was always invited to express an opinion as to the transport of these visitors, for the Lieutenant had been forbidden by his own bosses to provide any transport except for US personnel and information. Several times I was obliged to counter requests by French officers and officials in favour of rankers who were really sick or wounded. My friend Sgt Loerscher, of my own CA of the 2nd Battalion, was one for whom I was able to make a legitimate plea. Years later I learnt that he had written about the Legion in a Swiss newspaper and said that an Englishman, Sgt Murray, had saved his life by getting him on to an American plane when he was suffering seriously in China.

Early in June, on the day before I was to leave the base, the Lieutenant came to tell me that we had been invited to the Vice-Consulate to celebrate the official birthday of King George V and would I be so good as to speak on my experiences of Indochina. I was lent a dinner jacket and we were taken by Jeep and found some thirty people gathered there. We had a fine time with good food and plenty of wine to drink; the very things that I had been dreaming about during many a day, for I had abandoned my tee-totalism many years before. My speech flowed on for a good hour but it was well-received and several came to carry on the conversation until close on midnight when it was decided to call it a day. Suddenly, someone among the few remaining guests realised that we had forgotten to toast the King. It was remedied forthwith, with many red faces and the Lieutenant and I returned to the base in his Jeep. Such is life in foreign parts. With a thick head I said goodbye to my American friends and was flown to Kunming on the next Dakota and had to answer many difficult questions put to me by the Intelligence Officer of the US Airbase without getting the Lieutenant into trouble. I do hope that I was successful.

I stayed the night in a Christian hostel in Kunming and the next morning was directed to the British Military Mission and went up the back stairs to be met by the Captain in charge. On seeing the state of my clothes which I had not been able to repair since leaving the Legion, he immediately pressed the buzzer and a beautiful blonde girl appeared from the office next door with English tea and biscuits which were most welcome. The Captain then took me to meet a Colonel in civvies at an office outside of town. He was Colonel Buchanan and we were to remain friends for several years. He asked if I would prefer a commission as Captain in the regular Army which would take some weeks, or even months, to come through, or to become a civilian officer, with the same authority as a Captain or even a Major, in Clandestine Intelligence. I wanted to get cracking straight away so I opted for the latter and signed certain commitments.

I had several days of instruction to put me in the picture, drank a lot of home-made gin concocted by a ginger-haired despatch rider from Cornwall, and rested. A few days later I was loaded on to a DC10 and flown over the Himalayas to Dum-Dum, Calcutta's airport and then down the Bay of Bengal to take command of a Training Camp for our agents who were to be dropped behind the Japanese lines in Burma and Malaya. This was a most interesting job and I felt well-placed to offer such training given my own personal experience in the region. It lasted until the end of the war in August 1945.

It was only when I arrived in Calcutta and took up my new life that I felt that I was no longer in the French Foreign Legion. But I knew that I was still a légionnaire and would remain so for the rest of my life.

10
Reunions and Remembrances

L ife in the Legion was extraordinary and the friendships forged in those extraordinary times will last a lifetime. It never fails to surprise me how far and wide the Legion and its members continue to travel and reach and there have been many happy and memorable reunions with former friends and colleagues. The majority have been planned and organised but others have been quite by accident, which only serves to emphasise the point that it is indeed a very small world.

I remember so plainly an occasion in 1946 when I was getting off the Underground train at Leicester Square in London. I turned my head just a trifle and saw a beret disappearing into the compartment I had just left. I told myself that it was impossible but nevertheless I turned back into the carriage as the doors were closing. I walked along towards the beret and slapped the wearer on the shoulder *"Sacré Tétaert,"* I said. *"Qu est-ce que tu viens faire à Londres?"* (What on earth are you doing in London?) It was my Belgian friend from the Legion, Alphonse Tétaert! His was a particularly interesting story.

He had joined the Legion just before the outbreak of war. Things were quite difficult in Belgium during the thirties and he had had a number of different jobs ranging from teaching European History at a junior school to passing a course at the Medical Institute in Antwerp to go to the Belgian Congo as a medic. But he could not settle on a job that suited him. One of his friends had expressed his intention of joining the Legion and Alphonse said that he would probably join him later. He had seen films about Adolf Hitler and he thought there was going to be trouble with the Germans. Then the romantic side of his character, and his friend's departure, made him decide to join the Legion. He would make something of himself. He was going to be someone.

We met during our posting at Sidi-bel-Abbès and, after I had left in early 1941, Alphonse volunteered to fight for Tunisia alongside those heroes fighting the Nazis. One day he was called in to the Colonel's office where he was introduced to Major Albert, a Belgian officer from England who had come to enlist Belgians into the Belgian Army. Before the British authorities would support them with money and war material, they had to number at least three thousand. Tétaert asked for fifteen days to think about the offer: England and the fight against the Nazis, or to be an officer in the French Foreign Legion with only the faint possibility of being in action anytime soon. He opted for England and the Belgian Army and with a dozen others he went to Algiers, wearing a Sergeant's stripes to await embarkation for Liverpool, via Gibraltar. On the quayside he was approached by a pretty lady who asked him if, as he was bound for England, he would give a letter to her husband who was in London. The name and address were on the envelope. He took the letter, shoving it into his pocket. After a long and dangerous journey, my friend finally arrived in London. He stayed at a Salvation Army hostel and as it was Sunday he decided that it was a good time to deliver his letter. He looked at it and found that it was addressed to Georges Dumont, Belgian Radio & TV, Eaton Square.

He found the place and asked for Mr Dumont who was delighted to have news of his wife. He told Tétaert that he had arrived at just the right time. Would he like a job with *Radio Belge*? When Tétaert said that he would very much like to try it out, Dumont took him along to Bush House to meet the Boss. He was accepted and taught how to do the broadcasts to the Belgian people on how the war was proceeding, with messages and information, to friends and relations of the Belgians in England. But before any of that could happen, the Director told him that his name Alphonse Tétaert was not a name for the radio; he would have to change it. A secretary at Eaton Place was asked to get together a dozen good Gallic-sounding names during the lunch break. When he returned he picked one from the hat where the slips of paper had been deposited. The name on the slip was Luc Varenne. Luc went on to be a well-known and highly regarded sports commentator.

So, it was a bizarre twist of fate that we bumped into each other on the London Underground on that day in 1946 and imagine my surprise and delight when I learned that he was over to cover the Belgium-England football match at Wembley. We carried on to Covent Garden which was the closest Underground Station to the hotel where they were all staying and there he introduced me to the Belgian football team. We had drinks and I was invited to go to Wembley with them for the match the same afternoon. I enjoyed it very much, sitting way up above crowds listening to my friend giving his commentary in his inimitable French to listeners in Belgium.

My good friend, Pyl, the Austrian and Legion PT instructor remained a life-long friend too. He married a Countess in Paris. Together with General de Cockborne and their families, Pyl hosted my wife Beryl and me on a great many occasions over the many decades since the war. Often joining our little reunions was another good friend Jean Stockman. Jean had been in the 3rd Battalion of the 5th at Yen Bay in Tonkin, some eighty miles or so from Hanoi, and we often met playing football against each other. We also did the Corporal's and Sergeant's Promotion School together. He was the main radio-operator during the Great Retreat from Hanoi to China and rendered very important services. When he returned to France in 1945/46 he went to his native Austria as a Lieutenant with the Control Commission where he met and married Madeleine. After the war, they retired to Paris and Jean began to sell cleaning materials such as brushes, polishes and cloths. One day he told himself that this was not his scene; he would make the materials himself and get other people to sell them for him. Jean was of Jewish parentage and soon found a small, empty factory where he could set up shop. He then recruited a work force composed almost entirely of war-disabled persons to make all the cleaning materials he required. In France, apparently, at the time, no Government charges or taxes were incurred when employing disabled people and Jean rapidly collared a sympathetic market for his products and became very rich. He even came to visit me in London before I got married and years later drove to Bath in an old Rolls Royce.

I also remember Jean coming alone to Hyde Park Gate in the late fifties to present a scroll to Sir Winston, together with a fine watercolour of a légionnaire by my old friend of Sidi-bel-Abbès times, Andréas Rosenberg, with whom I had co-operated in painting the refectory of the *Musique*. I took Jean into the lounge where Sir Winston was sitting in front of a log fire. They shook hands and Jean handed over the painting. The Old Man was visibly moved and we each had a scotch and soda. Jean told me later that shaking Sir Winston's hand was the greatest honour he would ever have; he was a *Chevalier* of the French Legion of Honour.

The informal reunions among friends have provided me with reasons for holidays to last a lifetime and I consider myself lucky in having always been able to travel and look up old comrades when I do so. But it was not until fifty years after my joining the Legion that I was to attend its own Remembrance Day commemorations at the Legion Headquarters. So, it was in 1987 that I was to make the train journey from Paris to Marseilles with my wife in the renowned *Rhodanian* travelling at more than 80 mph, to attend the annual Camerone Day celebrations at Aubagne. Camerone Day is the Legion's most special day as it marks one of the most important battles in the French Foreign Legion's colourful history. All regiments have their own particular, more formal acts of remembrances and memorials to their fallen comrades. The Legion is no exception and the story of Camerone Day and the Monument of the Legion to its dead, around which Legionnaires parade, are stories that deserve to be told.

Night and day four bronze sentries stand guard patiently on the monument. Work began on it in 1929 when a disused quarry of onyx was found about fifteen miles from Sidi-bel-Abbès and Colonel Rollet, commanding the 1st Regiment of the Legion since September 1925, obtained permission from the Governor-General in Algiers to exploit the quarry gratuitously. He had conceived the idea of a monument to the légionnaires who had died for France and for the glory of the Legion. Company Sergeant-Major Salini, with Corporal Glass as his deputy was put in charge of the work which was to be carried out by thirty légionnaires from the Pioneer Company of the Regiment. They were all specialists in working with stone and marble.

The cost of the work was estimated to be in the region of 600,000 francs which was about £1,250 in those days. The money would be raised by each soldier, from the most senior Colonel to the most junior second-class recruit, each giving up one day's pay for four years. There was also some assistance from societies and communities in Algeria and in 1929 the famous concert orchestra of the Regiment, under the direction of my old friend Captain Paul Aka, made a very successful tour of the country to complete the raising of the amount required.

The names of the Légionnaires and other persons, about 30,000 altogether, who had contributed to funding the project, were placed on a list to be sealed within the monument. Ex-légionnaires in associations throughout the world were not asked to help but were requested to conserve their funds in order to pay the expenses of representatives who would then be able to attend the inauguration ceremony at Sidi-bel-Abbès.

500 cubic metres of concrete were necessary to support the monument,

for the Vienot Barracks had been built on marshy ground and water was not too far away under the surface of the hard-packed top-soil, rocks and cement originally laid down years before.

The cenotaph itself was to be 30 feet long, 23 feet wide and 10 feet high. The first stone was laid by Lieutenant Colonel Forey, great-nephew of a Marshal of the 2nd Empire, and the doyen of the Legion at the time. The date was 8th October 1930. Just six and a half years later I stood in its shadow listening to an NCO explaining why it was there.

While these preparations were going on, four superb giants in bronze were being made in Paris by the sculptor Pourquet, modelled from designs by the well-known painter, Mahut. They are considered to be Pourquet's best work. Each was some 10 feet high and destined to stand guard round the base of a terrestrial globe on which were to shine the immortal battlefields on which the Foreign Legion Regiments had fought with such glory. The first of these guards represented a Légionnaire during the reign of Louis Philippe, with épaulettes on his shoulders, baggy trousers and képi, carrying an 1822 model rifle as used in the conquest of Algeria (1840–1883) and he is the ancestor of the real-life légionnaire, the hero of Miliana, of Constantine, of Spain and Dien Bien Phu. The second guard, with his back to the first, wears the Crimean medal on his greatcoat, with its front flaps well raised to free his knees while marching, loose trousers with legs encased in gaiters (replaced by puttees in both the French and British armies at a later date for the sake of economy), a so-called 'leather stomach' of huge cartridge pouches, épaulets and a *képi* pulled well down on to his ears so that it stayed on despite khamsin or sirocco, with an elongated visor to shelter his eyes from the glare of the African sun. The rifle he carries is an 1842 model as used at Sebastopol and Magenta. This soldier has an impudent Imperial beard which, in a way, dates his epoch for it is certainly the silhouette of Captain Danjou and recalls the heroes of Camerone. The third soldier standing there also wears the greatcoat of the légionnaire, but he wears the Colonial *topi* like I myself wore when first I went to Indochina. He carries a Gras rifle of 1874. General Bruneaux himself sat for the beard, for his own is legendary. This légionnaire personifies the peaceful warrior of numerous expeditions across the seas during the 3rd Republic, which began in 1870 (the 4th began in 1946) to Dahomey, the Sudan, Madagascar and Tonking, in Indochina. Lastly, there stands the ordinary soldier of the Front Line Regiment of the French Foreign Legion, the légionnaire of General Rollet, ground-sheet across his chest, carrying a 1916 musket and wearing the typical French Adrian First World War helmet. He also seems to be carrying the torch of glory to show the path of duty to young recruits joining the ranks of new companies of the Legion.

Once the models were completed, all that remained was to mould the statues by pouring seven tonnes of molten bronze and transporting the huge results to Algeria to be erected on their respective plinths at each corner of the monument. A gantry had first to be raised to lower into place the hollow sphere representing the world, and it was then that a rather amusing incident took place. The sphere had to be bolted onto the base and this required the services of the smallest, thinnest légionnaire who could be found. He had to stand on the base while the sphere was lowered carefully over his head and shoulders and into place. He then fixed and made tight the nuts on the prepared bolts, following the instructions called to him by Major Maire who was in charge of the operation. He then tried to get out of the sphere via a small aperture that had been so carefully measured and cut into the bottom of the globe, just large enough for the légionnaire to squeeze out. It was never discovered if everyone had been too sure of the young man's suppleness, or if his proportions had increased due to the heat and the excitement of the operation, but in any case it took well over an hour to get the poor fellow out. The Major, by that time just as hot and frustrated as the légionnaire, was so happy to see the lad back on *terra firma* that he gave him a 100 franc note, a considerable sum when one realises that in 1937, when I joined, we were paid 1 franc, or a halfpenny, a day, and told him to go and cool down in the canteen. The Major himself then painted in, with gold paint, those parts of the sphere where the Legion had fought and lost so many of its soldiers, while the statues themselves were hoisted into their allocated positions. The Monument was completed on 10th March 1931, the anniversary of the date when the Legion was created. However, the most important date for the Legion is that of the famous Battle of Camerone, 30th April, and so the Centenary of the Royal Decree was eventually celebrated on 30th April 1931.

On the day when the Cenotaph was finally unveiled, it seems the entire population of Sidi-bel-Abbès gathered along the Boulevard de la République; the troops were in review order and delegations from ex-Légionnaires Associations from most countries in Europe were there in force with their flags, too. In the grandstand were gathered the civic authorities including the Mayor of Sidi-bel-Abbès, Prince Louis II of Monaco, who served in the 1st Regiment of the Legion, the Generals Guillaumat, Vandenberg, Colombat and Stanley Ford the American Military Attaché to Algiers. The British Colonel Etherton and Czech Colonel Kosik were also there. Honours were rendered to Monsieur Carde, the Governor-General of Algeria, who was accompanied by Franchet d'Esperey, that famous Marshal of France who had been Commander-in-Chief of the French armies in Salonika and had been responsible for the capitulation of Bulgaria and the expulsion of Austrian troops from Serbia. He commanded the Allied forces in Turkey until November 1920 and was created a Marshal of France on 21st February 1921. Elected to be a member of the French Academy in 1934, he died on 8th July 1942. He was a great hero and the Legion was most content to see him there to honour their dead.

Lieutenant-Colonel Forey, who had commanded the 1st Regiment between 1918 and 1920, and had remained in Sidi-bel-Abbès, was the President of the Monument Committee; he made a fine speech evoking the hard work accomplished by so many légionnaires and paid homage to General Rollet, the Premier Légionnaire of France. On completion of his speech, he handed the Monument over to Colonel Nicolas and the 1st Regiment of the Legion; the grand tricolour flag of France was unfurled to the sound of trumpets as the *Marseillaise* rang out over that vast concourse. Thus, that wonderful monument came into existence and every soldier salutes it as he passes; every civilian is expected to raise his hat.

After 1962, when Algeria became independent, the Foreign Legion was obliged to leave Sidi-bel-Abbès and moved their Headquarters to Aubagne, a town of some 30,000 inhabitants situated behind Toulon and Marseilles in the south of France near the mouth of the River Rhone. I wonder what scenes were enacted when the Legion left Sidi-bel-Abbès? When one enters the Vienot Barracks at the new Headquarters today, one is faced with a replica almost of the old scene in Algeria, except for the absence of the trees that used to give us some measure of protection from the blazing sun during parades – but I still remember it all with great satisfaction.

The Battle of Camerone is the most significant event in the French Foreign Legion's history. It took place in Mexico on 30th April 1863. A Legion company led by Captain Jean Danjou and comprising just 65 men, was attacked by around 2,000 Mexicans. They refused to surrender and fought until their ammunition ran out, by which time only three combat-ready legionnaires were left. The body of Danjou was returned to France, including his prosthetic wooden hand which replaced the one he had lost in Algeria in the 1850s. Although the strategical consequences of the Battle of Camerone were quite insignificant it nevertheless became the symbol of perfect courage and supreme sacrifice for the Legion and as such Camerone Day became the accepted day of Remembrance for the entire Legion. It was Napoleon III who ordered that the name of Camerone should be inscribed on the Regimental flag and standards and the names of Captain Danjou and the Lieutenants Maudet and Villain to be engraved in letters of gold on the walls of the Invalides Hospital in Paris where Napoleon's remains are interred (actually it was not until 1949 that the order was carried out and a plaque commemorating the event was unveiled on the wall).

However, that first Camerone Day parade took place on the 28th April 1906, and was thanks to a Lieutenant François, in command of Ta Lung, a small fortified post on the Chinese frontier, who had received news from France that the Cross of the Legion of Honour had been bestowed on the flag of the 1st Regiment of the Legion stationed at Sidi-bel-Abbès. He immediately ordered his men to clean the post most thoroughly and then on the 30th April he had them parade in front of him attired in their very best uniforms. The Lieutenant then addressed his men evoking past battles and sacrifices of the Legion that had led to the Regiment being granted this signal honour. The idea took hold and once it received the approval of Colonel Rollet, that great stalwart of the Legion, the First Légionnaire of France, its permanence was assured and now a parade is held, tales are told, special meals are cooked and much wine is drunk, on the anniversary of Camerone, wherever a detachment of the Legion may be, however small.

Captain Danjou's wooden hand is now the prize exhibit in the Legion Museum at Aubagne but once a year, on 30th April it is taken out, and still in its glass case, is carried during the Camerone parade there, escorted by the Pioneers of the 1st Regiment of the Legion wearing their distinctive white doeskin aprons, white covered *képis* and with axes over their shoulders.

In 1987, when my wife and I attended the Camerone Day celebrations, we were transported back in time and were treated to a most memorable occasion that neither of us shall ever forget. As I stood in the warm Spring sunshine, with my medals on my chest, the memories of my time in Algeria, Morocco, Indochina and China all came flooding back; the good times as well as the bad. There is no doubt in my mind that my time in the Legion not only defined me as an individual but also provided the very skills that were so valued and appreciated by my later employer, Sir Winston Churchill. The Legion, and the friends I made whilst serving in it, developed and championed those qualities that my dear family had instilled in me from a young age: those of loyalty, courage, a thirst for adventure and a strong desire to do the right thing. Serving in the French Foreign Legion during the Second World War was a time of vast extremes: friendships and learning, travelling to exotic and beautiful places which a boy from a mining village in County Durham might otherwise only have dreamed of. It was also the time of global conflict and I witnessed suffering and destruction to last a lifetime. But my time in the Legion prepared me, as best as anything could, for a life that demanded to be lived to the full, to the max, with integrity and with honour. And for that I will be forever grateful. So it seems I have come full circle and finish as I started this book: *Vive La France! Vive la Légion!*

Acknowledgements

My very sincere thanks go to:

Simon Murray (author of *Legionnaire*) for writing the delightful Foreword to Dad's book.

To Andrew Mitchell (author of *The Tigers of Tonkin*) for allowing me to use several unique photographs from his collection.

To my sisters Aileen Pengelly and Yvonne Sutton for their help in researching and reading through the manuscript.

To my wife Carolyn for her support and for drawing the caricatures of Winston Churchill and Charles De Gaulle that appear on page 6.

To my friends Ian Bailey, Nick Groom and Paul Rafferty who gave me great encouragement in the early stages of this project.

And finally to Ian Strathcarron, Ryan Gearing and Lucie Skilton at Unicorn Publishing Group.

Bill Murray

Index